The speed of life in the 21st century can be overwhelming but taking a calmer, more measured approach to the creative process can help you find new joy in the experience of making – and to produce textile art that is personal, sustainable and beautiful.

Slow Stitch is a much-needed guide to adopting a less-is-more mind-set, valuing quality over quantity, and bringing a meaningful and thoughtful approach to textile practice. Claire Wellesley-Smith introduces a range of ways in which you can slow your textile work down.

Take inspiration from textile traditions such as American quilting and patchwork, Kantha techniques, mending and darning, and Japanese Boro by working with what you already have, repurposing old textiles, re-piecing fabrics and building up texture with stitch. Use natural dyes from local leaves and plants to produce colours in thread and fabric that are more in harmony with the local environment. Harness the calming repetition of hand-stitch rhythms to explore your materials, make connections with other artists, be more aware of the creative process and rediscover the simple pleasures of making.

Richly illustrated throughout, and showcasing work from other international textile artists who work in this way, this is a truly inspirational book for those looking to reconnect with their craft and to find a new way of working.

Slow Stitch

Slow Stitch

Mindful and contemplative textile art

Claire Wellesley-Smith

BATSFORD

First published in the United Kingdom in 2015 by
Batsford
1 Gower Street
London WC1E 6HD

An imprint of Pavilion Books Company Ltd

ISBN: 9781849942997

A CIP catalogue record for this book is available
from the British Library.

20 19 18 17 16 15
10 9 8 7 6 5 4 3 2 1

Reproduction by Colourdepth, UK
Printed and bound by Craft Print Ltd, Singapore

This book can be ordered direct from the
publisher at the website: www.pavilionbooks.com,
or try your local bookshop.

Distributed in the United States and Canada by
Sterling Publishing Co., Inc.
1166 Avenue of the Americas, 17th Floor,
New York, NY 10036

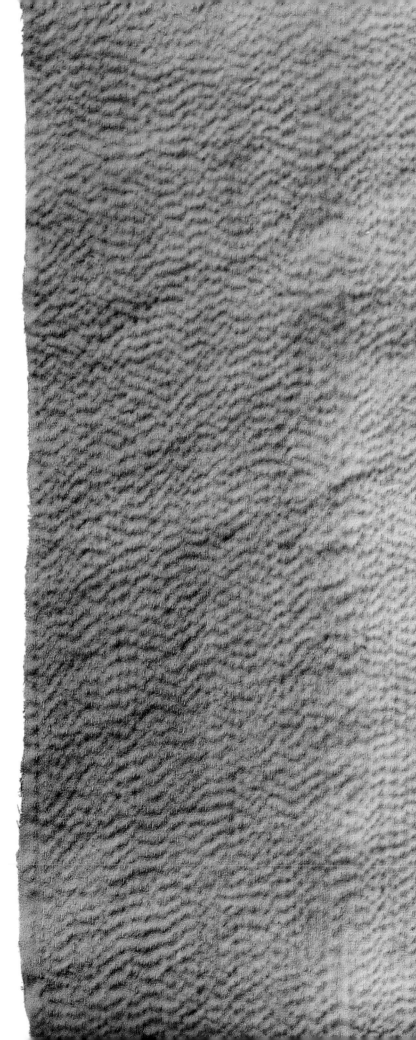

Contents

Introduction

The speed at which we do something – anything – changes our experience of it.
The Tyranny of Email, John Freeman

This book explores a 'slow' approach to stitching on cloth. The pleasures to be had from slowing down processes are multiple, with connections to ideas of sustainability, simplicity, reflection and multicultural textile traditions.

The idea of a Slow Movement has been applied to many things, but all look at slowing the pace of life and making a deliberate decision to do so. It is a philosophy that embraces local distinctions and seasonal rhythms, and one that encourages thinking time. In craft terms, I see a slow approach as a celebration of process; work that has reflection at its heart and skill that takes time to learn. By slowing down my own textile practice, I have developed a deeper emotional commitment to it, to the themes I am exploring, and to the processes I use. In the community-based stitching projects I run I have noticed the benefits that this way of working can give to participants. Simple, contemplative activities can be convivial too, creating non-verbal conversations through making.

The scope of textile art is huge. There are always new things to try, techniques to learn and products to buy. While it can be difficult to step away from diverting new experiences, self-imposed limits can bring a meaningful and thoughtful approach to your textile practice.

This book uses simple stitching techniques and traditional practices. It looks at choosing to use re-purposed materials and minimal equipment, and explores slow processes that allow thinking time and create a real connection with the object you are making. It has project suggestions and resources that will help towards making a more sustainable textile practice, and has examples of inspirational work from textile artists who work in this way.

You may find in using this approach that 'less is more', and that your slow textile projects become more personal and sustainable.

Right and left: *Slow Square* (2014). Naturally dyed threads on linen (40 x 40cm / 15¾ x 15¾in).

About me

I have come to this slow approach to textiles through a non-conventional route. I studied political science and had a career in community engagement and advice work for many years, often working with people who were experiencing crisis in their lives.

I grew up in a household in which things were made; my mother was a wonderful seamstress and knitter, a textile project always on the go, and she passed her skills to me. My grandmother was a professional machinist and dressmaker, who worked from the age of fourteen to help support her family. In my family, talking was mostly done when accompanied by making. I watched my grandmother knit a jumper for me as a student, fully engaged in all the conversation in the room and simultaneously completing a newspaper crossword. When I went to college to do creative textile courses as a new mother, I started to see connections between my own stitching and making, that of my female relatives, and in the communal support shared by my peers in the classroom. Gradually this developed into my main work, still based in community engagement but nowadays through my textile and teaching practice. My strongest interest is in connections: how do we connect to each other and how does the universality of textiles help us to do this? My approach includes archive-based research looking at the social history of textiles; exploring family stories through textiles and working on projects that aid understanding of personal and community history through textile making. The thread that pulls this together is a strong belief in the process, and I believe that the slower this process is, the more beneficial it can be both for individuals and communities.

Right: A detail from my stitch journal (see page 94).

Below: The view from my studio.

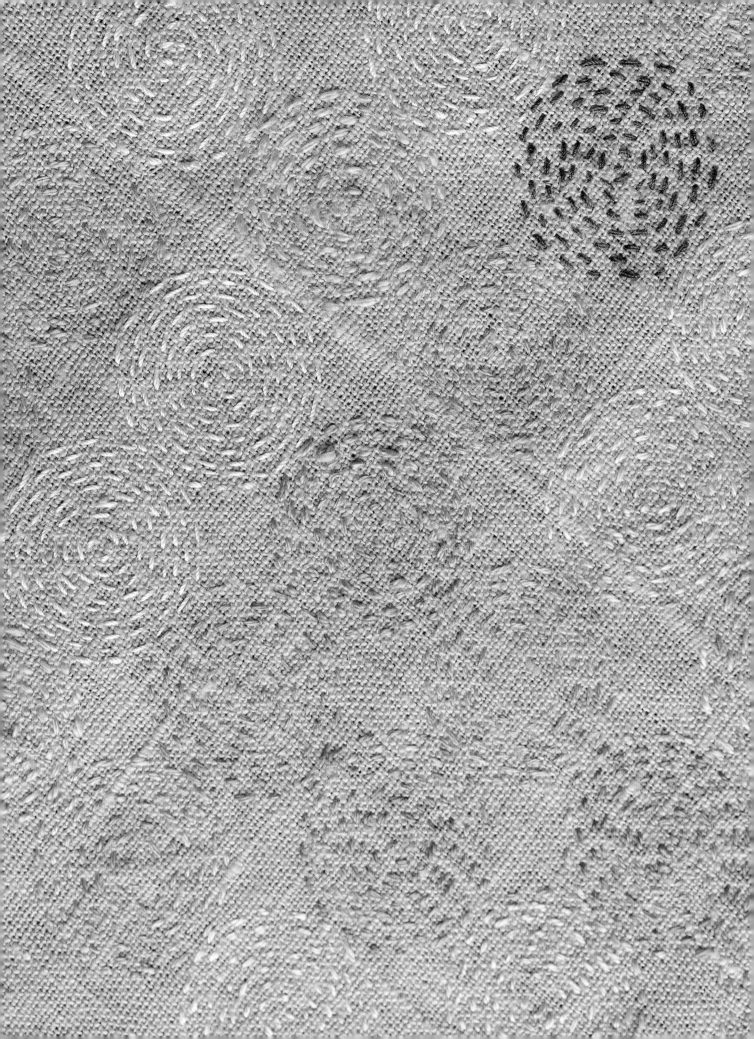

Part One:
Slow

What is the Slow Movement and how does it relate to textiles?

The origins of the Slow Movement can be traced back to the mid-1980s and the beginnings of the Slow Food Movement in Italy, started by Carlo Petrini. This began as a protest against multi-national fast-food companies and became a concerted campaign that encouraged sustainable local production, awareness of heritage, and strong connections to local culture and community. Carl Honoré's 2004 book *In Praise of Slow* broadened out these concerns, defining the Slow Movement as a cultural revolution against the notion that faster is always better. In the book he writes, 'The Slow Movement is not about doing everything at a snail's pace. Nor is it a Luddite attempt to drag the whole planet back to some pre-industrial utopia [...] The Slow philosophy can be summed up in a single word: balance [...] Seek to live at what musicians call the *tempo giusto* – the right speed.' And on his website Honoré goes on to explain, 'It's about seeking to do everything at the right speed. Savouring the hours and minutes rather than just counting them. Doing everything as well as possible, instead of as fast as possible. It's about quality over quantity in everything from work to food to parenting.' The Slow Food Movement has led to other Slow movements, including 'Slow Cities', aiming to encourage calm living places attentive to residents' needs and quality of life, and 'Slow Fashion', described by Kate Fletcher in her book *Sustainable Fashion and Textiles* as being 'about designing, producing, consuming and living better'. In the US, the idea of 'Slow Cloth' has been expounded by Elaine Lipson, an artist and writer with a background in the organic-food movement, who linked the principles of the

Right: *Field Work (Yellow)* (2012). Naturally dyed and pieced using repetitive hand stitching (35 x 15cm / 13¾ x 6in).

Slow Food Movement into a manifesto for textile making in her 'Slow Cloth Manifesto' article, published in *Textiles and Politics: Textile Society of America 13th Biennial Symposium Proceedings* in 2012 and also online at digitalcommons.unl.edu.

The speed of life in the 21st century can often be overwhelming. Life is relentlessly busy, but this is not a new phenomenon. In 1875, W.R. Greg wrote an article called '*Life at High Pressure*', much quoted at the time, bemoaning 'a life lived so full [...] that we have no time to reflect where we have been and whither we intend to go'. Around the same time, William Morris and makers within the Arts and Crafts Movement were consciously returning to pre-industrial processes, including the use of natural dyes and handloom weaving, despite the wide availability of faster, modern alternatives.

The issue of speed has preoccupied artists, too. The artist and weaver Anni Albers, writing in an essay titled *On Design* in 1939, talks of the 'indecision due to speed, the acceleration of processes, the rise and fall of ideas'. Now the digital age means that we are bombarded with information: emails and other notifications appearing on our phones, the pressing idea that we might 'miss out' on some vital news or update if we don't check now. The thing that I have become most conscious of is the number of interruptions in the day that come from external digital media and how long it then takes for me to regain my concentration after I engage with them.

The availability of ideas and inspiration, and the connections that can be made using online resources, are a fantastic facility for artists. However, I am increasingly interested in having a more measured approach to their use and this in part is due to my interest in the Slow Movement.

Working on textile projects in community arts settings has also drawn me towards the idea of slow processes. I have worked on a number of long-term arts and health projects with adults experiencing mental-health distress, and the two themes of connection and reflection have come to the fore again and again. I see a slow approach to stitch and textile projects as an enriching process. Simply thinking about your choice of materials offers an opportunity for reflection, to take time over the choosing of them, and to reflect on these choices as you work with them. This approach to the creative process can offer a calm space to engage meaningfully with materials and process and also with the people you may be working with. For me, the social context of textile making and production is key to this process. When you understand how things are made, where they were made, and why, you have a greater connection with them. The process of making by hand means the maker has a relationship with the object being made because he or she physically engages with it.

Using hand processes for textile projects is by nature slow. The real pleasure for me is the process, the doing and the getting there. David Gauntlett, writing about craft in his book *Making is Connecting*, describes it as '[the] satisfaction of making sense of being alive within the process, the engagement with ideas, learning and knowledge which come not before or after but within the practice of making'.

Above: Detail of *Field Work (Yellow)* (2012).

Sustainability and resource efficiency

I see a slow approach to textile projects as a low-impact approach. Reflecting on your projects and taking the time to consider the way you are working and consuming sits uncomfortably with products that are purchased at the expense of others' wellbeing. The textile industry is heavily entwined with environmental issues and the working conditions of those who work within it. For consumers in the West, the majority of textile production is now hidden from view, with poor labour practices mostly invisible to the consumer. Textile and garment production involves the cheapest and most flexible labour in some of the least regulated workplaces in the world. Many textile workers don't earn a living wage, and they work in unacceptable and dangerous conditions.

Issues around the production of raw materials include the use of pesticides in growing cotton, emissions to water and air from synthetic fabric and fibre production, and the huge demand on water supplies and non-renewable energy resources for production generally. In the UK we send 1.2 million tonnes of textile waste, much of it good quality, to landfill or for incineration every year. Of course, most of this waste is generated through the purchase of cheap clothing and textiles for

Left: *Field Studies* (2012). Naturally dyed, pieced and hand-stitched samples (10 x 20cm / 4 x 7¾in).

the home. However, I see the 'fast fashion' habit as akin to some of my old creative textile habits – do I really know what I am consuming? What are the impacts? An audit of my studio cupboards reveals small quantities of many different products, but with a large proportion lacking in mindful consideration of my purchasing power. What could I do if I approached it differently? Later in this book I will make some suggestions about sourcing materials that have better traceability, allowing us to engage with processes and materials that have less environmental impact. These are connected through the use of natural resources, local colour and place-based making. This process of working has its challenges but is more in tune with the idea of the lifecycle of things, offering to give the discarded a second life and showing the inventiveness that can go alongside re-use projects.

Above: Details from *Field Studies* (2012).

Locality and localism

Slowness gives you eyes in your feet and can be a catalyst for the senses.
Just a Little Run Around the World, Rosie Swale Pope

A key tenet of the Slow Movement involves a focus on localism – local production, local identity and consumption of products from the local area. I like the way that this can be linked to a common working process of artists, that of 'placeness', which is all about the relationships that can be made between art and site, bringing the local environment to the fore. Textile artists can bring multiple interpretations to the same site. In my practice, I have made a deliberate decision to be more observant of the things that go on around me in my local community and environment. I have tried to see my location and the places I visit in my daily life as 'slow stories'. Moments, events, marks left on a place, the things people did there and do there now, and the materials connected to places can be imbued with a sense of that place. Getting outside and walking familiar pathways give myriad ideas for my work, teaching and community-based practice. Nature is very important to me and there is a strong sense of both permanence, in the built environment, and of impermanence, as I observe the daily changes each season brings.

In community projects that explore heritage and memory, I encourage dialogue by engaging participants in textile craft projects. These sessions use conversation, the handling of cloth, fibre and use of local dyes, and

Above left: *Allotment Walk* (2011). Local plant dyes on reclaimed fabric (20 x 25cm / 7¾ x 9¾in).

Above centre: Weathered fabrics collected from my garden.

Above right: Small, regular hand stitches embed weathered cloth into a background cloth.

the generative activities associated with them. Meaningful contact within the group and a safe environment for sharing personal and community stories and histories are a hoped-for outcome. Sessions like this made me look afresh at the local area in which I live, give greater consideration to the impact on the landscape, of the people who lived here before me – and consider how this influences the way I work now. There is uniqueness in every place, whether urban or rural, coastal or inland, and you might use your slow textile projects to explore a place's unique qualities. You could look for all the possibilities that a local approach to textile-making can give – using local cloth or fibres, local weeds or other plants, and local water for dyes. This approach not only gives appreciation to seasonality as you become aware of the small, everyday changes going on around you, but it can create a sense of place literally from the soil beneath your feet.

Abigail Doan

Above: *Cornucopia* (2014) by Abigail Doan. Found fibres with handspun and dyed wool.

Abigail Doan, a US-based textile artist, explores themes of localism and locality through her work. Slowness is an integral part of this process. She writes on her blog, 'Slowing down is ironically a better way for me to examine my ideas about what seems essential for making headway in the studio and beyond.' Using found fibres – recycled textiles, old clothes, handspun and dyed wool, and what she describes as 'fibre flotsam' from her life – she creates sculptural forms. She also incorporates natural elements, be it plant material or other botanical specimens, from the place. These are explorations of slowness through materials and the place they were found or came from, and are a celebration of time and of the hand made.

I use natural dyes in many of my projects and often my washing line is full of samples from different plant-based dye baths. When gardening, I sometimes come across escapees, pieces and patches of cloth that blew away and have ended up weather-beaten, covered in green films, sun lightened in patches. I like these damaged, imperfect cloths, with their variations of colour and inadvertent prints from the earth or plant materials decorating their surfaces. I have also begun to enjoy the prospect of finding them and knowing that they will be different every time. In *The Textile Reader* Jessica Hemmings writes of textiles being '... a hostage to their own fragility – unlike metal and stone, the lifespan of the textile is not dissimilar to that of our own bodies: newness, gradually replaced by wear and tear until worn out.'

Below: Fabrics weathering slowly outside the studio.

Natural rhythms: cyclical and seasonal practice

Below: Seasonally gathered plants for dyeing projects are used for stitch projects like this in the colder months of the year.

In my community-based practice, I have had the opportunity to engage people in projects that tap into cycles of nature. Several 'seed to fabric' projects gave participants the opportunity to engage in the journey of seed to plant to dye and then on to collaborative stitch-based projects. Based in the North of England, in an urban area that was once dominated by the textile industry, it is interesting to think about how daily life has changed since the beginning of the Industrial Revolution. Prior to this, the cycles of the seasons were very much observed, a natural tempo of a rural economy – planting, growing and nurturing, harvesting, hibernating. The Industrial Revolution changed the way we perceive time, so that it is no longer shaped by seasonal rhythms. This quickly changed daily life as well as working practices. In some workplaces, there were even clocks made that measured productivity as time: a two-faced timepiece in a Preston silk factory was connected to the watermill that powered the machinery. The first clock face showed the time while the second one showed 'lost time' if the wheel did not turn quickly enough, and this time had to be made up at the end of the working day.

In a global economy shaped by units of production, time is no longer thought of in the same way. Now, in our post-industrial society, we have moved far away from a model of 'time as nature' and into a digital world in which everything operates in an increasingly fast way, characterised by quick transactions and ready availability of most things. As Abigail Doan wrote in January 2011 on ecosalon.com, 'I have always linked crafting with one's hands to agricultural activities ...' She believes that people are drawn to [craft] activities 'as they allow one to feel environmentally grounded and connected to a place. Understanding a start-to-finish process of any craft-based activity mirrors life cycles and the rhythms of nature'.

I try to be aware of seasonality when planning community projects and in the way I work on my own textiles. The warmer, lighter months are spent nurturing dye plants and engaging with the outside environment. The processing of colour is best done at the time of traditional harvest in the late summer and early autumn; the textile work, hand-stitching and making, through the winter. Change in the seasons is embraced in this way, cyclical patterns echoing cycles of nature and the reassurance that this will be repeated.

Above: Scraps of weathered fabric carefully stitched to keep them intact.

Lotta Helleberg

Lotta Helleberg is a Swedish-born artist based in the USA. Her current work focuses on documenting nature in her immediate surroundings. She uses local plants for fabric dyes and also includes them in natural printing techniques, such as leaf and eco printing as pioneered by Australian artist India Flint. The resulting impressions are incorporated into art quilts, textile collages, artist's books and other objects.

She says, 'Almost all my work relates to nature, botany, and the fragility of our environment. I use motifs and images directly derived from nature, either from contact prints, or from natural dyes and pigments. I try to finish my pieces by hand whenever possible. Hand-stitching connects me with the materials and enables me to weave together layers and sections in ways that are not possible with machine-stitching or other methods. The slow, methodical stitching of selected areas also creates new patterns and textures that reveal themselves as you go along. Working with my hands is an indirect way to honour both my subject matter and century-long traditions of hand sewing that came before me.'

Below: *Reminiscence / Rose* (2013) and detail (shown below left) by Lotta Helleberg. Eco print and hand stitch. Photographed by Stacey Evans.

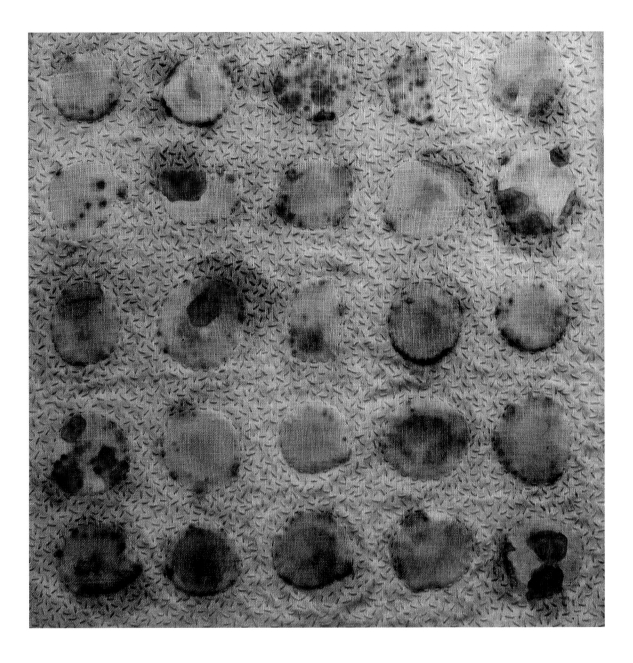

Alice Fox

Above: *25 Beer Bottle Tops* (2014) by Alice Fox. Linen, found metal and hand stitch in cotton/silk.

Alice Fox is an artist working in textiles and printmaking. She builds up layers of found marks, print and stitch to imbue her pieces with a sense of place rather than a pictorial representation of it. Of the piece *25 Beer Bottle Tops*, she says, 'This quilt-like piece is made using found bottle tops collected from the street in various locations. They were trapped between two layers of linen and held in place, surrounded by hundreds of seeding stitches. Once the hand stitching was complete, the whole piece was made wet with tea, allowing the trapped rusty metal to react with the tannins in the tea and producing a whole range of tones and marks on the cloth and stitches. The marks develop slowly. There is no control over where they become more intense than others. There is just the chemistry of the metal, liquid and air working together to stain the fibres that they are in contact with and doing it in their own time.'

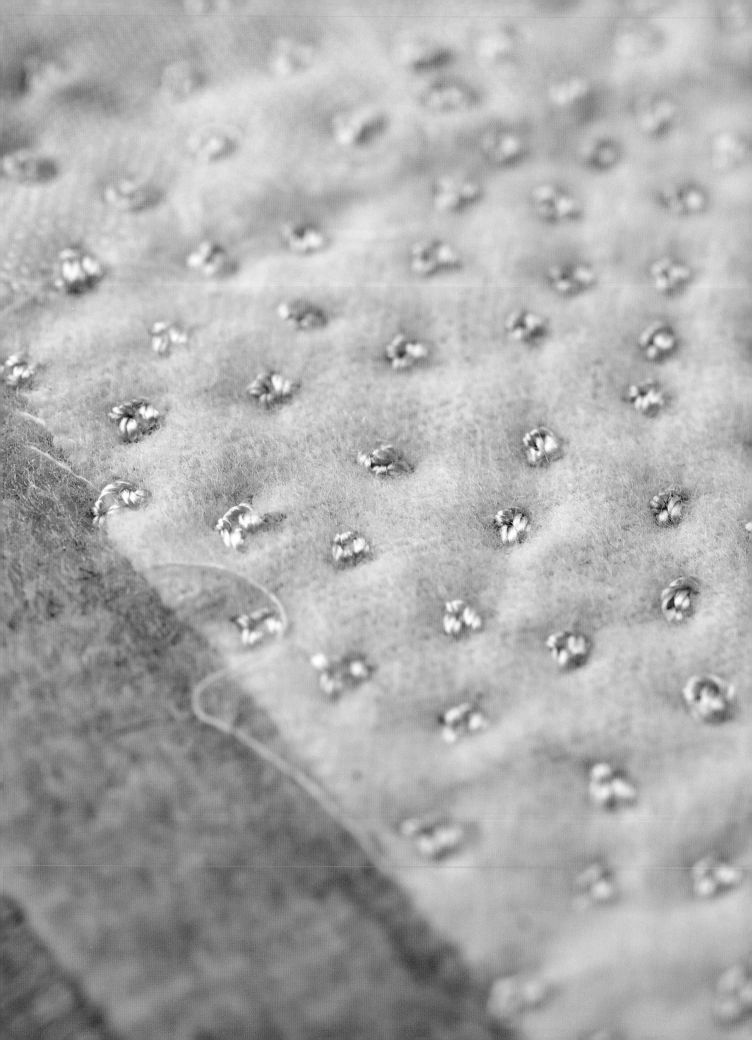

Part Two:
Materials and techniques

Limit setting: less can be more

My students have heard me describe the 'archeological dig' I embark on at the end of each term. I can pinpoint exactly what we were covering in our classes by looking through the stack of books, handouts and materials that build up on the table in my studio. In the evening class I teach, we cover many topics, but I have observed that often the techniques that use minimal equipment and easily found materials are the most popular, and inspire the most conversation and sharing in the group.

The riot of promise that can be provided by textiles, and the many techniques you can employ when working with them, can be a double-edged sword. Yes, variety is the spice of life, but what about the overwhelming feeling of having too much choice? I tend to find this happens when I walk around the big annual textile shows. There are so many ideas – new products, colours, patterns, projects and exhibits – to inspire, yet it can be so stimulating that it is hard to know where to start with it all. Textile artist Jae Maries put it very well in 'The World of Embroidery' July 1999, Vol. 50, no. 4: 'There are so many techniques to try that you can easily become wooed by the technique itself rather than asking yourself if this method of working is really appropriate for your subject matter. The individuality of the creative embroiderer becomes obscured by technique and that personal voice that will distinguish your work from your neighbour's in an exhibition will be smothered by the technique itself ... we may dabble forever and never get focused, like the butterfly fluttering from one seductive flower to another.' This is not a criticism of technology or of work that celebrates the possibilities of multiple processes. However, I find that my own voice is more authentic when I set myself limits.

Right: Worn patchwork scraps, ready to reuse.

What's in the cupboard? Using what you have

Some years ago, in my own practice, over-faced by the amount of stuff I'd collected – particularly fabric remnants, vintage scraps, leftovers from previous projects, and samples, washed, folded, stored 'just in case' – I resolved that I would draw a line and try not to accumulate any new materials. It gave me the opportunity to reassess the types of fabrics I use and look anew at what I already had. My community projects benefited from some of the excess – shiny synthetics, heat-sensitive plastics, multi-coloured yarns from old knitting attempts, quilting cottons that were bright and seductive when I bought them. I was left with cloth and threads that hold some meaning: repurposed from favourite old clothing, old quilt scraps with meandering joining stitches, worn fabrics ripe for over-dyeing, woollen blankets with a lovely weight to add my own stitches to.

The result of this 'fabric edit' has meant that I am working with familiar cloth and this gives me the most pleasure. It has also helped me to explore the way I engage with the materials I use and the reason I have chosen to keep and re-work them. The more you use them the more you recognize their potential and sometimes limitations. For me, imposing limits has built and inspired creativity and has given me new ways of approaching materials, rather than continuing to try out the latest textile trends.

Collecting and sourcing materials

I write from the lucky position of someone who has collected textile materials and equipment for years. I also inherited the workboxes and fabric collections of many female relatives. However, if you are starting slow textile projects for the first time, you may be looking for your own cloth, fibres and other materials to begin your work.

Fabrics

Right: Previously used in a quilt top, these collected patchwork hexagons can be given new life in a slow textile project.

Using repurposed fabrics gives you some idea of the provenance of the materials. Cloths that have been worn with use have a pleasant, soft handle. They also have a resonance, carrying their own slow stories. They are quiet objects, but working with them can give them a new life or purpose. When deciding what to use ask yourself: How does handling them feel? How do they speak to me?

Wool

Wool blankets – find them in charity shops. They re-dye beautifully and are also excellent to use as a ground for adding stitch or other materials to. I have also used them as the wadding in quilting projects.

Woollen knitwear – look out for the 'Woolmark 100%'. This means that you can gently felt the garment to make a strong fabric for cutting and reassembling.

Woollen jackets and suiting – strong in backgrounds and great to add hand stitching to.

Cottons and linens

Household linens – embroidered tray cloths and antimacassars are still widely available at car-boot sales and in charity shops. I like to find those that are past conventional use due to stains or mends and that invite reworking in some way.

Larger domestic linens – tablecloths, curtains and their linings, bedspreads. These can all be used as larger backgrounds for pieced work or could be overdyed or printed to create a new working surface.

Handkerchiefs – These can be wonderful to use as a 'self-contained' background piece of cloth. The hemmed edge, sometimes decorated with lace or pulled-thread-work detailing, can frame new stitchwork beautifully.

Old clothing

Check the label and look for natural fibres. These offer more possibilities for re-dyeing and are nicer to use in stitch projects than synthetics.

Men's shirts – ideally look for 100% cotton rather than polyester mixes (and remember to save the buttons).

Larger-sized women's dresses, shirts and skirts to deconstruct – these give you larger pieces of fabric to work with.

Threads

Below: Old threaded spools with silk and cotton – high quality and enjoyable to use.

Look out for old spools of thread. They tend to be made from natural fibres rather than polyester mixes and this means that they have a better finish. For a project making slow-dyed threads, and altering bought threads see pages 44–45.

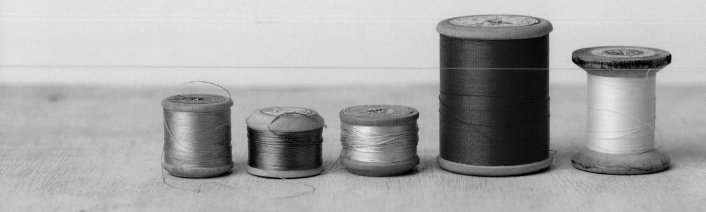

Where to find old materials

Above: New organic fibres, fabric and thread.

Start in your own cupboards, weeding out linens or old clothes, then try second-hand and charity shops and markets. Specialist textile sales sometimes include dealers with collections of very worn cloth at reasonable prices – Victorian and Edwardian chemises, baby dresses and old handkerchiefs often stained or heavily mended.

Scrap stores are also great places to find usable cloth. These are social enterprises, sometimes set up by charities who collect and reuse unwanted materials from businesses and manufacturers and then resell them at very low prices.

New materials

As discussed earlier in this book, textile production is a resource-heavy business. It can be difficult to establish the provenance of materials and to consider the many ethical and environmental issues when purchasing new fabric. However, there are some options available.

Buy local

What is made in your local area? You may live somewhere that has a tradition of textile production. I am lucky to live in a city that was once known as the wool capital of the world, where fabric and locally produced wool yarn is still relatively easy to get hold of. On a smaller scale, you may find that contacting your local guild of Spinners, Weavers and Dyers gives you an idea of where to purchase local cloth and you could perhaps meet the maker too. It may even give you an opportunity to engage in some collaborative working practices.

Eco fabrics

There are now several retailers that specialize in sustainable fabrics. These include hemp (a highly productive plant, pest resistant and easy to cultivate), bamboo (absorbent, fast-drying and naturally anti-bacterial, from a very fast-growing plant), shoddy (re-spun wool fabric made from recycled wool waste), organic wool (sourced from farms that use sustainable working practices) and peace silk (made where the silkworm is allowed to live out its full life cycle rather than using conventional processes that kill the silk worm). These retailers will also sell cotton. Look for organically produced fabric with Fairtrade certification. Organic cotton production uses none of the harmful chemical pesticides used to generate conventional cotton: production is, therefore, good for the producer, the natural environment and wildlife, and creates a better income for the worker. The supplier I use can tell me about the family who makes the hand-loomed cotton in India, as it comes straight from the weaver.

Upcycling and re-using old projects

Right: Unpicked, resewn, restitched indigo patchwork pieces, embedded into a new surface with seed stitch.

We all have pieces in our sewing boxes or cupboards that never made it: samples that were never finished or completed work we didn't like enough to use or display. Re-using old projects can give you an opportunity to reflect on past work and consider the changes in your practice as you re-work and make something new. You can work with old projects as new work or you could continue to add to your original ideas for the projects and extend them. You could consider the following words when you begin: Unpick, Rework, Develop, Adapt, Revisit, Permanence, Impermanence. Consider the ways of reworking listed on the following pages.

Overdyeing

Overdyeing fabrics, plain or patterned, can give pieced-together or patched work a homogenous and completely different look. A simple and resource-efficient way is to use a tray for dyeing (cat litter trays work well for this). This gives you a contained area to work in and uses less water and dye. It also means you can control the way that the dye works on the fabric. Bulkier fabrics, when crammed into a tray, will take dye in a less even way for a patchier finish; smaller pieces will have a much more even result.

Applying dye using a squeeze bottle or simple paint brush means you can control exactly where you want the colour to be strongest. I use natural dyes in my own practice, but you could adapt this method for your preferred dyeing medium. For some simple natural colour ideas see the section about hand-dyed threads on pages 42–46.

The 'orphaned' pieces from an English paper-pieced quilt from the 1930s in the photograph (shown right) have been reworked using a gentle dip in an indigo dye bath. I like the way that the blue shade has unified the print and pattern of the piece. I used the smallest offcuts to repiece into a new sample with simple seeding stitches pulling the scraps together (see photograph on page 35).

Natural bleaching

Light and white fabrics respond to the sun to bleach out stains and lighten generally. Hang wet fabric out to dry on a sunny day (add lemon juice to your soaking water to speed it up) and you can brighten light-coloured cloth.

Right: Patchwork pieces overdyed with natural indigo.

Adding other fabrics

Above: Old hexagon
patchwork densely
stitched on to wool.

Think about using some of your collected materials such as repurposed clothes, household
linens, or old scraps of fabric to add to a surface. Reassembling fabrics on to a new backing cloth
gives some stability when you are stitching. I like to use old wool blankets as backgrounds when
working in this way. Use pins, repositionable fabric adhesive spray or simple tacking stitches to
position the work. If you are using additional fabrics, find ones of a similar weight to one another
as they will easily merge together into a new surface when you begin to stitch.

In the photograph (above) an abandoned piece of my work, created using very worn hexagon
patchwork and small swatches of fabric, was overdyed using walnut dye and has been remade
through dense stitching on to an old wool blanket.

Whole clothing

Above: From *In Search of Green* (2013) by Hannah Lamb. Botanical print on repurposed textile with hand stitch.

You could consider using a whole unreconstructed piece of clothing as a background for additional patching and stitching.

Artist Hannah Lamb in her installation *In Search of Green* recorded time and place by drawing with stitch and making marks on cloth. The pieces build upon old garment sections, pieced together, as a reference to the human form. Nature prints and found objects become incorporated into textural surfaces that reference specific walks or seasonal changes. These garments are a personal and sensuous response to landscape during early spring.

Dense stitching

Closely worked, repetitive stitching adds to the solidity of a piece and can give it new decoration. You could also decide to use this method to obscure some original decoration on a piece of cloth or to minimise the joins in pieced work.

Using scraps of fabric, or a cut-off piece of the project you are re-using, try out different repeated stitches such as fly stitch, running stitch and seeding stitches to see the different effects they make.

In the photograph (shown left) the tiny assemblages of men's cotton shirting and old embroidery on linen were over stitched to unify the surface.

Left: Recycled men's cotton shirting and old embroidery were assembled on a linen backing cloth. Note the different effects a repetitively worked stitch can have. From top – running stitch, seeding stitch and fly stitch.

Mandy Pattullo

Mandy Pattullo's work is based on collage techniques. She patches and pieces together fabrics and is drawn to pieces of cloth that have a patina of use and show evidence of the hand of a female needleworker of the past. She sources and uses vintage quilts and other fabrics that are then upcycled into her own work. She describes this as her 'thread and thrift' vision and this includes her desire to work only with old and passed-down materials. Her collages combine piecing and appliqué techniques with hand stitch and the incorporation of various found objects and recycled embroidery.

Left: *Full Stop* (2012) by Mandy Pattullo. Hand pieced patchwork of vintage material with stitch (35 x 18cm / 13¾ x 7in).

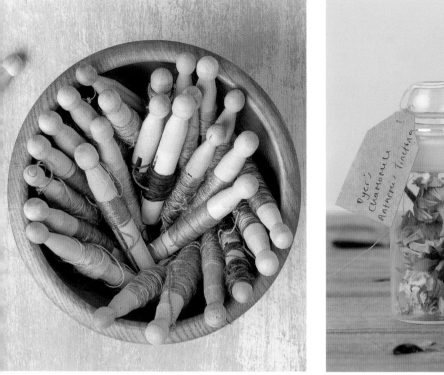

Slow-dyed threads using local colour

Natural, locally gathered dyes have a different quality from their synthetic counterparts. Plant-based colours have a complexity of tone that make shades particularly agreeable when used together, and are firmly rooted in the place they came from. The colours mirror the landscape, and the colours of the place inspire the cloth and stitches.

Using a slow approach to colouring fabric and thread is a key part of my practice. I like to use locally sourced dyes and nurture my own dye garden at my allotment. This section of the book looks at a local slow approach to colour, how to use easily obtainable natural colour and how to produce a palette of slow-coloured threads for your textile projects. There is an inherent slowness in this process – in the time it takes to achieve the colour on the threads. In my own practice, it also includes the whole process of growing the plants that produce the dyes, but there are many easier ways to collect and to find local colour.

In much of my work, I use ordinary hand-sewing thread, usually old, and I have a particular love for 'silk style' glacé cotton or I use threads that I dye myself using plant materials. I do this for a number of reasons:

- I can create a connection to the other fibres used, often dyed in the same dye-bath.
- I find that natural colour can be less flat and uniform, and harmonizes with other colours in a different way from synthetic dyes.
- I can create my own muted palette of colours.
- I can use dyes until they are completely exhausted (meaning that the colour is used in its entirety) and at this stage create blended and variegated shades on my thread skeins.

Above left: Threads dyed using locally grown or foraged dye plants.

Above centre: Locally produced dyestuffs from a community project.

Above right: Dyer's chamomile at the allotment.

Permanence and impermanence

Most natural dyes require a fixative, or 'mordant', that acts as a chemical link to bind the natural colour to the fibre. When I use mordants, I choose those with the least environmental impact: alum, iron, oak galls, rhubarb leaves. However, I sometimes like to work without this process, knowing that the results I achieve will have a degree of impermanence – or, to use the dyeing terminology that they are 'fugitive'. When working with weathered samples (see page 21), I like the effect that exposure to the elements can give to the cloth or thread – be it fading by the sun or a wearing of the fibres.

Slow dyeing your threads

Materials:

A selection of clean, empty jam jars with lids
Small skeins of wool, silk and cotton embroidery thread
Alum mordant (if using)
Gloves for use when handling mordant materials
Rusty nails
White vinegar
Plant material or kitchen waste

Common plants to look out for:

Plant name	Part of plant used	Colour made
Walnut	Outer husk of nut	Brown
Rosemary	Leaves	Yellow
Tansy	Plant top (flowers and leaves)	Yellow
Dock	Root	Orange
Goosegrass / cleavers	Root	Pinks, reds
French marigold	Flower heads	Yellows, greens
Nettle	Leaves or roots	Green
Viola / pansy	Flower heads	Blues, purples
Acorn	Whole nut	Brown, black
Elder	Berries	Purples, pinks
Sunflower	Flower head	Bronze, bright pink

Colours even closer to home

An easy way to experiment with natural colours is to use what you have in your kitchen. I particularly like to use things before they head to the compost bin. It is a great end-use activity and can create subtle and interesting colours. All of the following make good dyes:

Kitchen waste	Colour
Coffee grounds	Shades of brown
Tea bags	Antique cream, tan
Onion skins	Yellow, orange, brown
Black beans (soaking water)	Blue
Avocado skins	Pale pink

Method:

1. Dissolve half a teaspoon of alum powder or granules in a little boiling water in a jam jar (swilling the liquid around the jar will help it to dissolve).

2. Add plant material to the jar and top up with water. The quantity of plant material that you use will affect the result. If you cram in lots of leaves or flower heads then make sure that you have room to add your threads to the jar.

3. Add your skeins of thread (pre-soaked). You may wish to weigh them down with a small pebble or other weight, so that they are immersed in the dye liquid rather than floating at the top. Screw the lid on (you can put a disc of waxed paper or jam jar disc to prevent mould on the surface before sealing).

4. Put the jar on a sunny windowsill or leave it outside and check regularly to see the thread shade. On a sunny day, the change in colour can be quite dramatic as the sun heats the solar bath. On cooler, dull days the process will take longer. When you remove the threads you can add the remaining plant material and liquid in the jar to your compost heap or around your plants if you have a garden.

Above left: Solar dyeing jars. From left to right – onion skins, buddleia flowers, St John's wort and woad seeds.

Above right: Coloured threads after solar dyeing.

Altering the shades

There are simple ways to alter or modify the colours produced in your slow dye jar.

Iron

Iron is a 'saddener' when used in a dye bath. To 'sadden' (a traditional dyeing term) a dye is to darken the eventual colour. When used in large quantities, it will create rich dark grey shades, dark browns and black.

To make your own iron modifier, mix 9 parts water to 1 part vinegar to make a vinegar solution. Add a handful of rusty nails and leave with the lid on for a week. The solution can be kept and added to your slow dye jam jars when required.

To 'rouze' or brighten a dye bath, again altering the shade, you could create a similar modifier this time using copper scrap, vinegar and water.

Overdyeing commercially dyed threads

To alter the colour of commercially dyed threads you could add them to your solar dye jars. An alternative method is to 'knock back' the brightness. Soak the threads in a strong solution of tea or used coffee grounds. Set your oven to its lowest setting and put the threads in to dry out on a rack. The heat and the tannin in the tea or coffee will darken and 'age' the thread.

Right: Commercially dyed embroidery threads with 'softened' colour after soaking in tea and oven drying. Clockwise from top – threads before dyeing, threads after dyeing with tea, and a sample showing the contrast in colour between the original threads and threads after overdyeing.

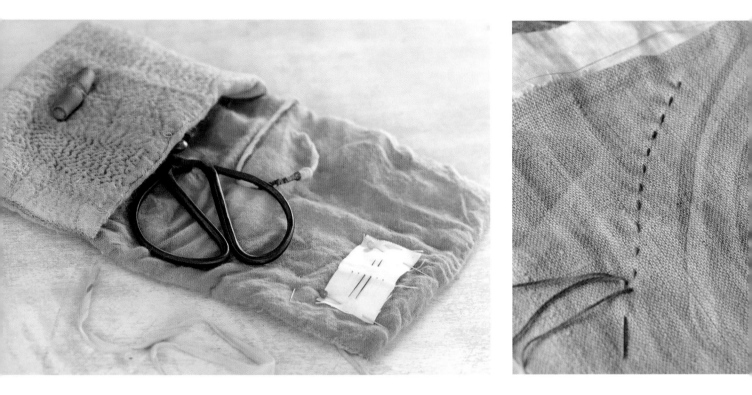

The right tools: equipment suggestions

Above left: Slow-stitched sewing wrap for essential equipment.

Above centre: Marking fabric using a wooden pottery tool – a needle would work too.

Above right: A selection of marking tools. From left to right – water-soluble pen, hera marker, pottery tools and wooden darning needle.

The Slow Food Movement encourages people to enjoy the process of sourcing and preparing meals. Part of this process includes the tools used when cooking, perhaps a good sharp knife that is easy to handle and works efficiently. In textile projects too, the tools we choose should be pleasurable to use, as they are an instrumental part of the way we transform our materials.

I have a few pieces of equipment that I keep in a quilted sewing wrap (and a mini version that I carry with me all the time, just in case I find an unexpected moment in my day to do some stitching). I also keep with me my notebook in a stitched removable cover, with ties so that I can add things I collect as I'm out and about and then keep securely wrapped up.

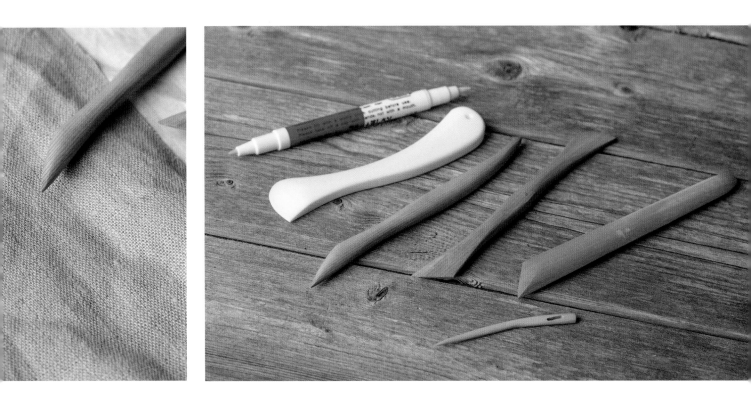

My sewing-wrap kit includes:

Sharp scissors – I take them to a local ironmonger to be sharpened.

My favourite needles (made by John James). My preference is for sharps, embroidery or quilting needles, depending on the project.

Marking tools – I have a variety that I use, depending on the fabric. I use them for sketching out a simple line. Water-soluble pen, hera markers, and my favourite – wooden pottery turning tools. When I don't have any of these tools, I find that I can mark a line to follow with stitches just by using the point of my needle.

Pins and 505 spray – When working with pieced backgrounds I use either pins from my pincushion or a temporary fabric adhesive spray to assemble and reorder my designs. When I am happy with the arrangement I apply large tacking stitches to hold the piece in place while I work on it. I use a fluorescent coloured thread for tacking. It saves anguish when pulling out later, as I never confuse these stitches with my more muted embroidery!

Simple stitches: getting started with hand-stitch rhythms

When beginning to stitch, I have been using a method that I find useful in getting to know my materials. This is a warm-up exercise of sorts. Using a plain woven linen fabric, I 'get to know' the surface I have chosen by only using that material – to work on and to sew with. I gently remove a thread from the edge of the piece and thread up my needle with it, then re-stitch it into the body of the fabric. As a result, the fabric grows and shrinks simultaneously and I am left with a more densely constructed section in the centre of the cloth and an unravelled edge. I can decide whether to pull threads out from the same place or to leave pieces between the rows of the warp threads visible.

This method may seem counterintuitive: why create and destroy at the same time? I think that for me it is a demonstration of exploring process for the sake of it. The end product is not the reason for doing it, rather it creates a head space where I can think and yet be fully engaged with the material I am exploring and this may lead to other creative ideas.

In the photographs (shown below and right) I extended this method by dyeing the edge of each cloth before I began, so that the indigo-dyed edge became indigo threads to sew with; these gradually faded as I continued to pull them out and stitch.

Right: Threads pulled from the indigo-dyed edge of a piece of recycled linen have been reworked into the body of the fabric.

Left: Detail of stitching with pulled threads on indigo-dyed cloth.

Stitch a square

Above: Detail of a stitched linen square.

Right: Student samples show the variety of interpretation using this simple exercise.

When teaching and exploring slow stitching methodologies with groups I sometimes use this exercise and find that it is useful in a number of ways:

• Starting to explore a reflective space.
• Establishing a rhythm.
• Understanding the many possibilities of a 'plain sewing' technique.
• Thinking about stitch marks as a kind of handwriting – everyone will have a different approach and leave a different mark.

Materials:

A piece of linen marked with a square: use a marking technique of your choice
Embroidery thread – just use one colour
A needle that you feel comfortable using
An embroidery hoop (if using)

Method:

1. Mark a square on to your fabric and begin to fill it using running stitch. You can do this in any way you choose using stitches of any length. The important thing is that you get into a rhythm that you feel comfortable with (for some ideas about running stitch and the different configurations look at the kantha section starting on page 60).

2. Take your time with your stitches and when completed take some more time to reflect on your sample and the marks you have made.

I asked students to complete this exercise and to share their reflections on the process. These included observations on the effect and look of the stitch on the fabric: 'Many wonderful effects can be produced by the repetition of this one stitch. I find the results amazing' and 'I enjoy the sense of colouring-in with thread, creating texture by changing direction so light falls differently on the thread. The weave of the linen suggested making shapes within the square and I wondered if starting in the centre and stitching out would be more unwinding and relaxing.' Student reflections also highlighted the therapeutic capacity of working in this way: 'I used this stitching – as I sometimes do – to cope with something that had upset me a few days earlier. I can see my agitation in the stitches but the process was calming and seemed to almost take the uneasiness out and into the work where I can look at it as something almost more understandable.' And, 'Calming. No pressure.'

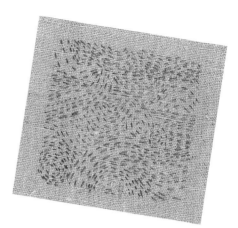

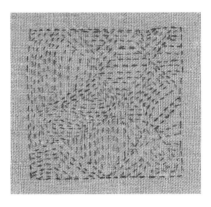

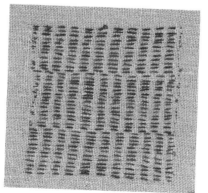

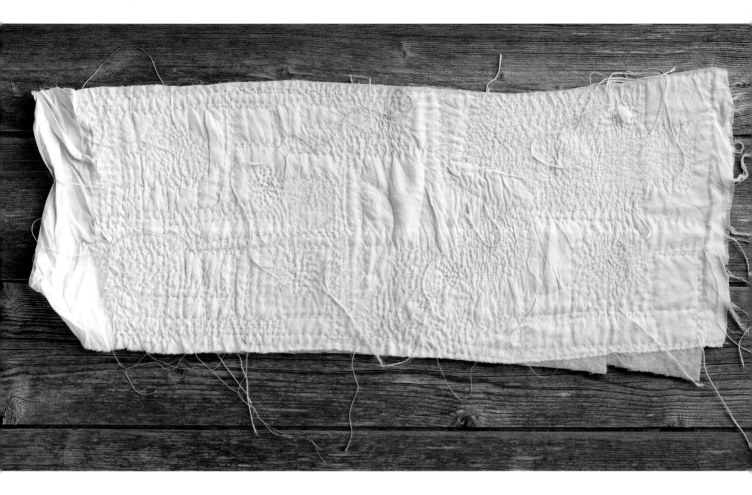

Above: Meandering white stitches on silk, like taking a line for a walk (60 x 25cm / 23¾ x 10in).

Explore the process:

You could repeat and vary the exercise on page 52 in different ways and it can be altered to try out different stitches.

The stitch: Think about other ways to use the stitch: sew from one side but use the reverse. Consider how you stitch – is it towards yourself, or away from yourself – does it make a difference? How does using a hoop alter the effect or your enjoyment of the process? Change the length of stitch, direction, regularity. What happens when you overlap your stitches? Try 'taking a line for a walk' and allow your stitches to meander across the cloth.

The fabric: Try the same exercise with a variety of different-weight fabrics. Running stitch is the most common quilting stitch. Try stitching through layers – how does this affect the process and the texture when finished?

The thread: Try a different weight of thread, a different type of needle, alter the tension of the thread as you use it, use double thread and compare with single thread.

Developing your stitches

An extension of the exercise on page 52 is to try different stitches and see how the use of them alters your process.

The examples in the photograph above show the differences that can be seen when using different stitches on pieced backgrounds. The fabrics used are the same, assembled in slightly different configurations – scraps of silk, brushed cotton, wool gauze all in their undyed state (these could be overdyed at a later time). Running stitch, fly stitch, sorbello stitch and seed stitch all leave a very different impact on the fabric and the texture of the cloth. The process of the stitching was also very different for each type of stitch. Because of this the rhythm and by extension the repetitious aspects of the work varied considerably. Knotting stitches are individual by design – each one must be completed before moving to the next. The process has less fluidity than, for example, using a stitch that uses a rocking motion, like running stitch. However, there is a certain method and timing that emerges as you repeat a format multiple times and this can be very pleasing and enjoyable.

Above: Four white-on-white samples. Simple pieced backgrounds with embedded stitches. From left to right – seed stitch, running stitch, sorbello stitch and fly stitch.

Below: Detail showing sorbello stitch using old buttonhole silk twist thread. This is a simple stitch worked in a square. When stitched very small it looks like a knot; when worked larger it looks like a cross stitch with a knot in the centre.

Part Three:
Cross-cultural activity

Universal traditions

Beverley Gordon writes of textiles being like signposts – personal, emotional, historical and cultural in her book *Textiles: The Whole Story: Uses, Meanings, Significance*. The universality of textiles and textile-making techniques mean that we can see traditions repeated, adapted, moved across continents, shared and modified. Textile objects often develop and change in an unmanaged way. A good example of this would be the tradition of quilting, which involves two or three layers of fabric held together to make a warm and decorative cover. Exploring the origins of American quilting traditions shows the development of the craft from English methods of paper-pieced patchwork that settlers took to the USA, as pioneers in the seventeenth century. The beautiful twentieth-century quilts produced in the rural community of Gees Bend, Alabama, demonstrate this. They are firmly grounded as items for use, created through the reuse of everyday materials including denim work clothes and animal-feed sacks. The makers developed block-piecing traditions from the early pioneer quilters, adding traditions from their own Afro-American culture alongside.

Personal and community connections and an appreciation of skill and tradition are a key aspect of the Slow Movement. As with food, we all have a relationship with cloth and a greater or lesser understanding of where it comes from, and how it relates to our heritage and culture. When I teach I sometimes ask students if they would like to share their earliest textile memory with the class or group. A wonderful collection of stories emerges around the table as people reminisce about the texture of a corduroy sofa and how it felt to touch it, candlewick bedspreads, the pattern on a relative's sari, the bobbles on a hand-knitted jumper, even the sensation of climbing into a bed made with nylon sheets. There is a huge diversity in how we engage with textiles, how they help us to remember and construct ourselves. Pausing to reflect on this in our own lives and in textile traditions from around the world can be a powerful thing.

Artist and academic Hannah Lamb has used textile archives in many of her projects and uses this research process of unearthing stories and narratives connected to the construction and use of material in her own practice. She says, 'Researching historical textiles broadens our awareness of the rich cultural legacy we work within. Learning about techniques from the past gives us a deeper understanding of our discipline and the wealth of possibilities that can be explored.'

This section of the book looks at some textile traditions from around the world. The techniques described are not intended to mimic or imitate traditional techniques, rather to explore their beauty, process and some of their history.

Right: Old quilt pieces from the author's collection. In the top quilt another older quilt has been used as wadding. These unearth more textile narratives about the people who made and used them.

Kantha

I keep a dorokha kantha quilt on my bed. The flexibility of the cloth, so well used, handled and manipulated means that the softened layers make it a comfortable and comforting thing to use. The multiple stitches give the fabric a draping quality. Worn sections when held to the light now reveal the fabric layered within.

Above: Dorokha and nakshi kanthas from the author's collection.

Right: Dorokha kantha from the author's collection, showing wear and patches.

The kantha quilting technique originates in Indian Bengal, now Bangladesh, but there are also variants found in Pakistan and India. References to the craft appear in accounts going back centuries and feature in fairy tales and folklore. These functional items were originally a product of a traditional culture where waste simply did not feature. Saris, lungis and dhotis, much washed and mended, would eventually be incorporated into kanthas – and these used as bedding, floor coverings and wrappings for devotional and other objects. Sheila Paine, in her detailed book *Embroidered Textiles*, writes of the kanthas of Bengal protecting 'all manner of precious things, such as books, the Koran, musical instruments, money, betel nuts, mirrors, combs and toilet articles.

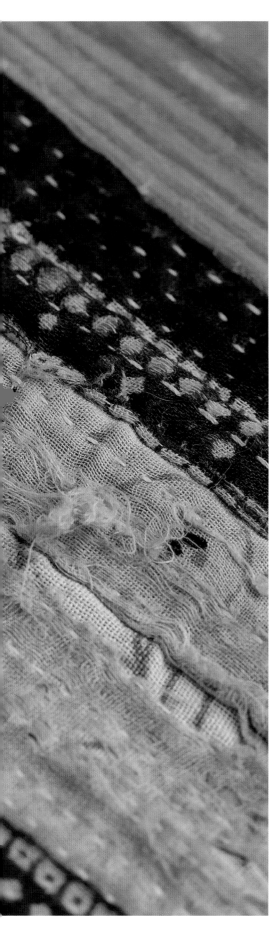

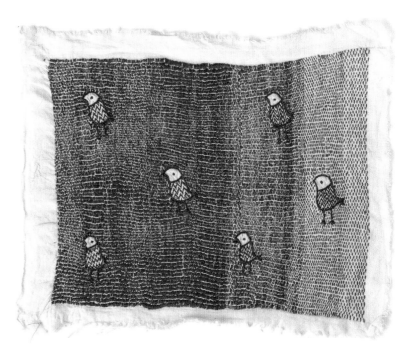

Their making is a ritual activity: for Muslim women Friday is an auspicious day to begin, while for Hindus it is a Tuesday.'

In functional dorokha kantha, layered pieces of worn-out cloth (usually patterned lungis or sarongs) were stitched together using simple running stitch to make a two-sided quilt. The layers of cloth would be secured and held in position with weights placed at the corners. The sides of the cloth would be tacked together to stabilise the work. Running stitch holds the pieces together so that the join between different cloths and patterns is hidden.

These functional items invoke intimacy and domestic use and demonstrate generations of women's work. In Bangladesh, old cloth is said to keep the user safe from harm and the softness of the worn cloth and solidity created through the simple stitching feels comforting to touch.

A development of this is the nakshi kantha, a more decorative technique that uses motifs drawn from everyday life, religious belief, nature and folklore. In this way they illustrate the rural life of the women who stitch them, becoming folk-art documents. Motifs of plants, people, animals and common domestic objects feature frequently – mostly outlined in backstitch before being filled in with running or darning stitch. Border patterns have developed mainly from running stitch but are also full of traditional symbols. These stitches were sometimes worked using threads pulled from the woven border of otherwise plain saris.

Kanthas are about memories and stories, connecting generations of women who made and repaired them through their simple stitches.

Left: The worn edge of this dorokha kantha exposes the layers of fabric used in construction.

Above: Contemporary nakshi kantha by Padmaja Krishnan, from the author's collection (32 x 25cm / 12½ x 10in).

Kantha technique

Above: Repurposed handkerchief with rhythmical kantha stitches.

The techniques used in kantha-style work are rhythmic and absorbing. Having explored a small square of running stitch as described on page 52–53, you may wish to extend the idea and work with some traditional kantha stitching patterns. The ideas shown here are not meant to replicate / imitate, but to introduce a style of working using repetitive stitch. Different ways of stitching, using simple patterns, are very effective when repeated and create an undulating, rippling effect on the cloth.

Materials:
Soft fabric, preferably cotton, although fine linen works very well (cotton lawn, fine muslin, well-washed sheeting or handkerchiefs). You will need enough to create three or four layers. An alternative is to use lightweight quilt wadding (wool or cotton would be best), although this is not traditional. If you are using this method, you will need to sandwich your wadding between two fine layers of fabric. You could use cotton scrim for a fine layer on the back.

Preparing the fabric
Iron the fabric and layer it together then tack around the edges and through the centre of the piece. A useful tip is to pick a tacking thread in a bright colour to avoid any mishaps when removing later.

Thread

Fine cotton threads or quilting threads. I love to use vintage cotton threads when stitching in this way. Look out for thread reels that say 'glacé' or 'silk finish'. Traditional kantha stitching would use white thread on white cloth for background areas, and coloured threads to make the detailed drawn images. Using self-coloured thread (the same colour as the background cloth) means that the eye will focus on the texture of the surface. A stronger or contrasting coloured thread, or indeed a variety of colours, draws the viewer's attention to the stitches themselves.

Running stitch is the most basic stitch used in kantha work. However, the method used to make it will alter the surface finish of the cloth.

Below: Tacking threads hold the layers together before stitching begins.

The kantha stitch

The characteristic appearance of a kantha is that the surface has a rippled effect. In *The Art of Kantha Embroidery*, Niaz Zaman writes that 'The principle of the kantha stitch is that the spaces between the stitches are larger than the stitches themselves'. When stitching the next row, stitch parallel to the previous row but let the stitches fall slightly behind or move slightly forward instead of alternating with the stitches in the preceding or succeeding rows. This method produces the rippled effect and a ridge-like 'wave' between the stitches (see figure 1).

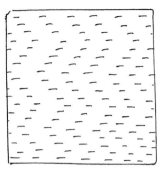

Figure 1

The darning stitch

In contrast to the kantha stitch, the darning stitch is more 'interwoven'. It is still made up of small running stitches, but this time deliberately spaced to alternate with the preceding and succeeding rows. The ripple effect is lost, but this stitch is very useful, for example, when unifying two pieces of cloth by stitching over a joined section. Running the needle through the cloth and making several stitches at the same time works well to gain this effect (see figure 2).

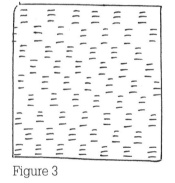

Figure 2

Pattern darning

Stitches are worked in close parallel to achieve this pattern. It is also used in some pictorial motifs such as leaves or wheels (see figure 3).

Working a square

Use your marking tool of choice to divide your square up with diagonal lines. Work each triangular section using running stitch, beginning in the centre and working outwards towards the side of the square (see figure 4).

Figure 3

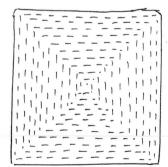

Figure 4

Right: Repurposed handkerchief worked in squares using (clockwise from top left) pattern darning, darning stitch, kantha stitch and a worked square.

Pat Fuller

Below and right: *For Dorothy Beniston* (2012) by Pat Fuller. Cotton thread on calico worked using traditional kantha-style border stitches (27 x 18.5cm / 10¾ x 7¼in).

Pat is an artist who I first met when she joined an evening class that I teach, having just retired from a long career in teaching. She found that learning about kantha-style stitching had a powerful effect on her, and she chose a subject that connected with close personal relationships. The work developed over time and was picked up in odd moments of reflection. 'The way the kantha-style running stitch builds up shapes and texture was compelling and taking time resulted in a piece that developed as I went along. I've gone back to the stitching skills I learned as a child, but I now add value to slowness, and I've gained this in later life.'

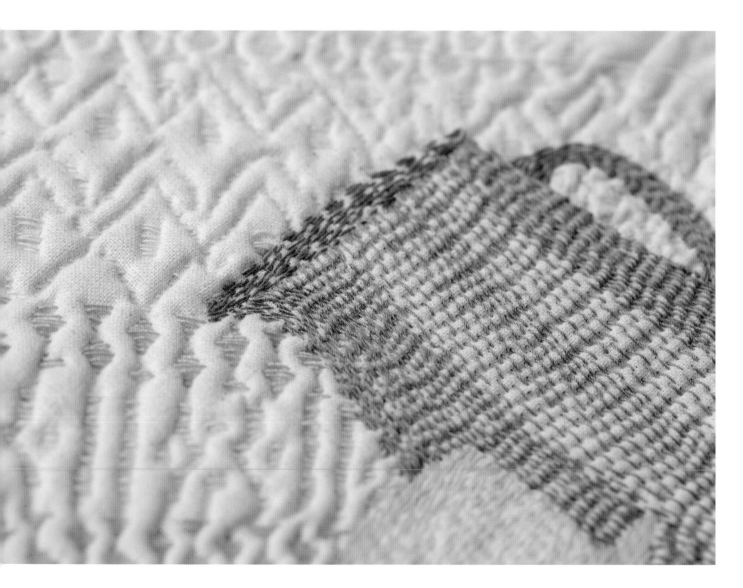

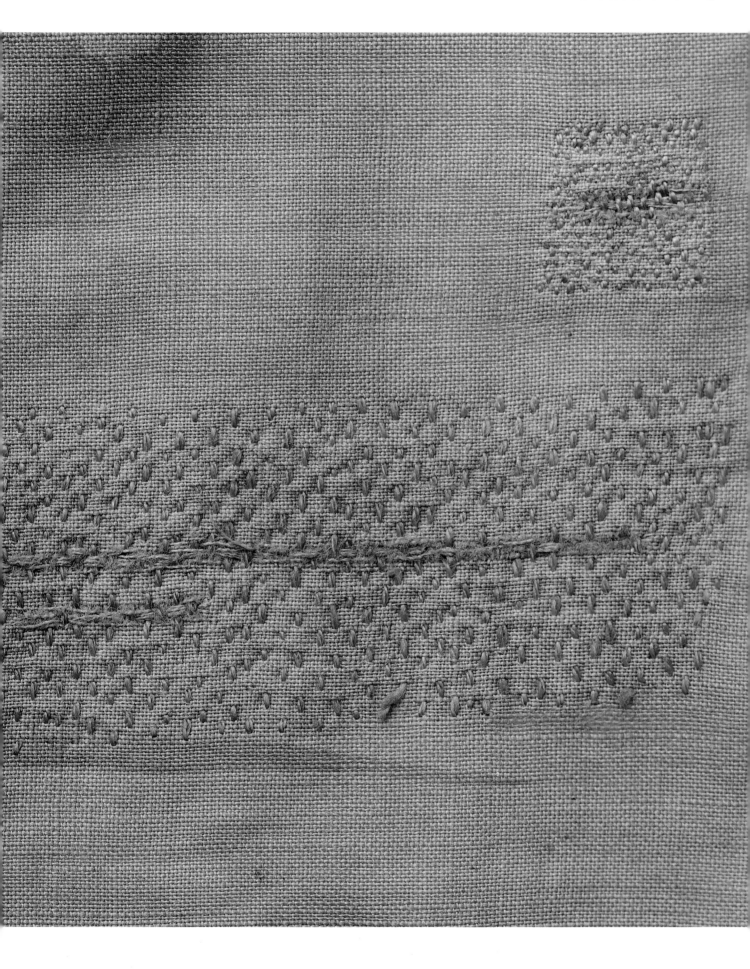

Mending revisited

You repair the thing until you remake it completely.
Louise Bourgeois: The Fabric Works, **Germano Celant**

Left: Invisible mending on an Edwardian chemise, from the author's collection.

Above: Detail from a 1920s Dutch darning sampler, from the author's collection.

Textile mending has become a seldom-seen activity due to the ready availability of inexpensive fabric and clothing. A sustainable textile future would suggest that it is essential to revive these skills and to value the things we buy, to give them longevity and to encourage a more ethical approach to our textile use. Being able to mend one's belongings can be an empowering feeling. Repair can add to the potential of an object, make it something unique and act as a creative challenge. Investing the time it takes to repair something gives you a different emotional response to it and it becomes personal to you in a new way. Plain sewing techniques can be used to reinforce or transform something and give it renewed purpose and life.

Mending creates a visible connection with an object or item of clothing and I like visible mending, as these kinds of marks become a narrative, illustrating how the item has aged. Looking at old textiles can be like reading them, the marks of stitches or darns like the previous owners' handwriting, the marks of wear a journey through the life of that fabric.

Mended things hold histories, and these are narratives of time. The patina that is created by the wear is often unseen in museum textiles where you mostly find the best-preserved (or least used) items. However, repairs show an emotional acknowledgement of the fragility of the material world and this is a powerful statement.

Practical and beautiful

Alongside the practical function of repair techniques, I find a real beauty to be found in the finishes and pleasure to be taken in the slow execution of the mend. Pattern darning, with origins in the vocabulary of mending, has more recently become a technique practiced due to its attractive and highly decorative results. Similarly, sashiko embroidery, with its eighteenth-century origins in rural Japan, began as a technique for strengthening clothes and household items to maximise their longevity. The recognizable white stitches on an indigo-dyed base cloth were later developed as a decorative embroidery technique.

I like to mend and I like to make my mending visible. A worn placket and pocket on an old linen work shirt of mine (shown in the photographs above left and above right) has been revived with faded indigo linen patches and some simple reinforcing stitches over the patches.

In the photographs shown right the patching swatches show simple ways of adding patches to worn fabric, working over and under the mend.

The added stitching demonstrates the difference when you minimize the mend by choosing a neutral coloured thread to reinforce the patch, as opposed to celebrating the use and wear of the garment using bright red.

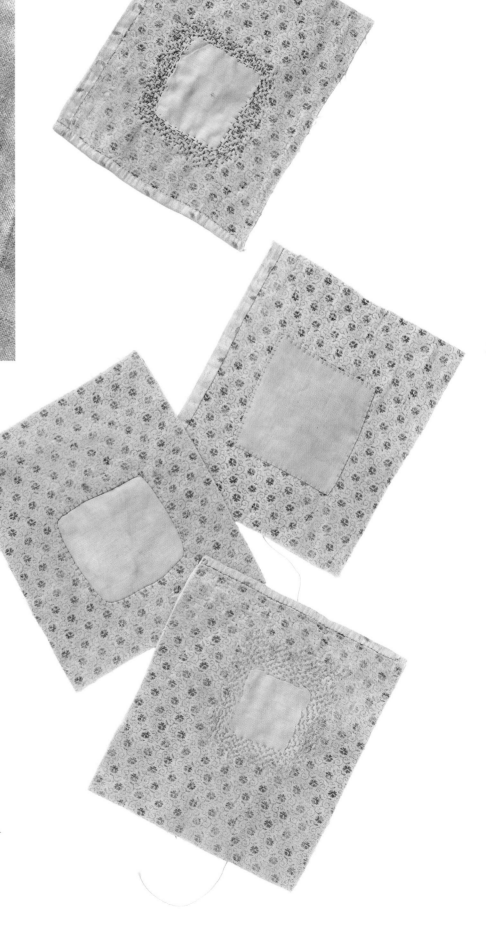

Above left and above right: Simply patched using indigo-dyed fabric, my linen work shirt is enhanced and can be used again after mending.

Right: Darning swatch samples. Patching ideas, from top – reverse appliqué patch with overstitched edges in red to create a visible mend; simple patch; reverse appliqué patch; reverse appliqué patch with blended stitched edges.

Emotional repair

My grandfather came from Hungary first to Australia, as a refugee fleeing the Nazi occupation in 1939, and then to England. Of the few things saved when he left his homeland was a piece of traditional Hungarian redwork embroidery, probably made for a sideboard or other piece of formal furniture. Photographs from my childhood show this cloth on the back of the sofa in suburban Sydney when he settled there with my grandmother. Later, after my grandparents had died, it covered my mother's dressing table. It is now in my sitting room, the pattern and faded red stitches something of a constant in my life. The marks of the maker are visible, stitched using thick

Left: Hungarian cloth, from the author's collection. Marked by use with stains and invisible mending, it carries family stories and memories (115 x 55cm / 45¼ x 21¾in).

thread; the back of the piece by no means perfect, but there the red thread is a far brighter hue, less faded by the sun as the cloth travelled around the world. And around the edges of the cloth, tiny darns and mends: the weight of the decorative blanket stitch around the linen has pulled at the warp and weft of the cloth, leaving it vulnerable to rips. When I look at it, and more so when I handle it, I think of the women, family I never met, and there is a strong feeling of connection. Through the work of their hands, and my understanding of the mending techniques and stitches they used, a piece of cloth made over a century ago brings us together.

Celia Pym

Above and right:
Hope's Sweater, 1951
(2011) by Celia Pym.
Moth-eaten sweater and
darning (30 x 40 x 3cm /
12 x 15¾ x 1¼in).

'I like to see how something is made, how it works. Darning is good at helping you understand an object; you darn it and you can figure out how it works, where it is strong and weak, how it was constructed, how it was used, loved.'

Mending and the process of mending, particularly of other people's clothes, is central to Celia Pym's artistic practice. The holes in clothes and the personal attachment to objects in our lives are explored as stories, the mends becoming part of the history of the garment and, correspondingly, the life story of the person who wears it. It is an emotional process that leads to a person wanting something mended. There is a story behind the need for the mend – it could be wear and tear, an accidental rip, a moth or age, and the mender learns about the garment, its construction and use as she or he mends it. Celia encourages the people she mends for to allow her to make the repair visible, using a brightly contrasting wool or material to execute the mend. She says, 'My thinking about slowness is that I am a slow worker (sometimes) and I like working in a way in which you watch something grow – which is part of the reason I think I work with textiles because knitting and stitching and darning grow; you add on to the last part. I also work with textiles because I relate to their softness, warmth, tactility ... Part of the pleasure I take in darning is looking at the smallness of a hole and thinking about how I will fix this hole but if the garment continues to be used that hole will inevitably grow (no darn is forever) and then that in fact the mending job is ongoing, the hole will need tending to again in the future, and this is slow work, a future job.'

Kate Bowles

Kate Bowles is an artist who uses recycled fabrics, papers and vintage haberdashery ephemera to make books and journals. She has made a series of fifteen darned books inspired by a collection of old linens and threads given to her by a fellow artist. 'I am very interested in using discarded and pre-used materials, and giving them status and value … so much of women's work is made invisible, thus I am thoroughly enjoying celebrating the darning by making it a feature of these case-bound books.'

Above and right: *Darned Books* (2014) by Kate Bowles. Case-bound books with recycled fabrics and hand stitch.

Japanese boro

There has been recent huge interest in Japanese boro – the heavily patched and mended domestic textiles from the rural north of the country, dating back to the nineteenth century and into the twentieth.

Sumptuary laws in Japan meant strict hierarchies existed in the country and these extended into the use of cloth and dyes. The rural poor would have had access only to homespun cloth made from hemp and flax, and would often have been involved in every stage of production: planting, nurturing and harvesting the fibres, then spinning, weaving and dyeing them. The dyes were limited to a few colours only – the distinctive and varied blues of indigo and also grey, brown and black.

The word 'Mottainai' is significant (and sometimes boro is referred to as boro-mottainai), as it is translated as 'too good to waste' and would mean that every scrap available was used until it wore out. Therefore, these textiles would make a journey that sometimes went from adult kimono to child's clothing, to being reassembled into a family futon, and finally into hearth rugs and floor rags. Distinctive sashiko-style stitching was used to patch, mend and reassemble pieces as they were reinvented for use, often through generations.

Above: Japanese patched indigo katazome, early 20th century, from the author's collection.

Left and above left: Heavily patched and darned shorts, early 20th century, from the author's collection.

Boro is an inheritance that far from being celebrated in Japan was seen as a visible sign of poverty and often shame. I can appreciate greatly the layered cloth, the hand stitching – often showing the marks of different makers, the infinite variety in the shades of indigo-dyed patches and the composition of these items in how and where the patches were applied. However, mostly this work speaks volumes about the dedication of women who battled to keep their families warm and the time it took them to do it. Daily use sometimes requires daily repair; these cloths tell us much more about the lack of re-use, and therefore the loss of historical narrative we have in our own domestic textiles today.

Piecing and patching

Patchwork and piecing techniques offer an opportunity to embed meaning into work. The connections you may have with the cloth used – the memories imbued in the materials, the stories you may have about them or maybe just the sheer enjoyment of the processes you may have already used on them, such as dyeing and printing, feel amplified to me as I choose, cut, piece and stitch them. Marybeth Stalp in her book *Quilting: The Fabric of Everyday Life* describes patchwork and quilts as 'meaning laden objects … women reach back through history to make connections to unknown women artists, who constructed quilts before them, and they leave messages embedded in their quilts for quilters and non-quilters in generations to come.' In community settings, quilt-based projects offer an opportunity to explore collective memory through the choices of cloth that participants make, how they engage with a process, and the communication and conversation that goes on whilst making. Projects that can be easily moved around, picked up and worked on, then put down again, and added to as and when, can be particularly useful in busy times.

I like projects in which work is assembled on to a foundation or backing piece of fabric. It offers an opportunity to patch and piece together fragments but gives them some stability, and means that the cloth is really solid to hold and you experience the whole cloth, as you manipulate it through stitching.

The basics of log-cabin technique are a good way to create pieced backgrounds for stitch using precious scraps of cloth. 'Log Cabin' was a popular type of patchwork in America and England, particularly during the late nineteenth century. The process builds outwards from a central square of material. This was traditionally red to represent the fire in the hearth at the heart of the home. Strips of material then build out from this centre, the corners overlapping.

The construction method means that it is possible to incorporate even the tiniest scraps of material, but also offers other ways of playing with the format of pieced backgrounds.

Right: *Pieced Green* (2012). Recycled, naturally dyed fabrics and hand stitch (38 x 20cm / 15 x 8in).

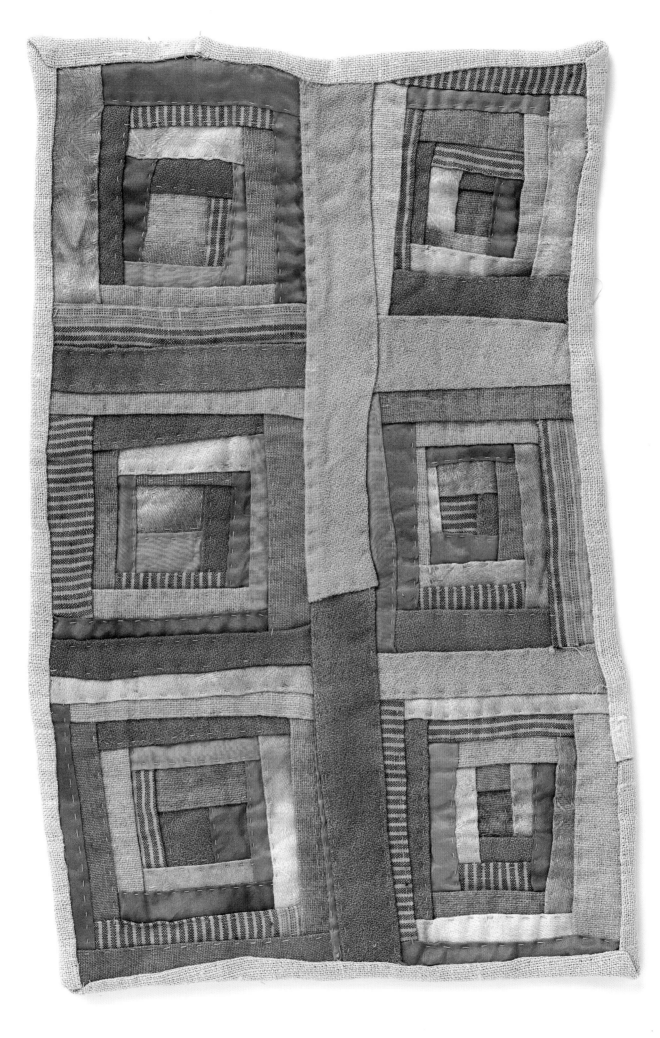

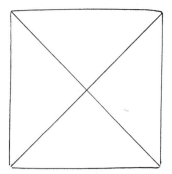

Figure 1

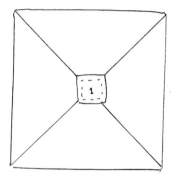

Figure 2

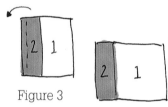

Figure 3

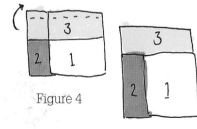

Figure 4

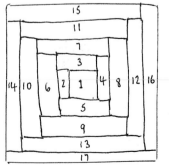

Figure 5

Log-cabin patchwork

Materials:
Pieces of calico or old sheeting for the foundation (background) fabric. Strips of cotton, silk, ribbons, linen or any other thin material for the piecing. Thicker fabrics with a stable raw edge need no seam allowance.

Method

1. Draw a square (make a template if you are making multiples) on to your background fabric and mark it diagonally – crease it or use your marking tool of choice (see figure 1).

2. Cut a small square of material and tack to the centre of the cross (see figure 2).

3. Cut the first strip and place it right side down on the centre square. Stitch 5mm (¼in) from the edge then fold back and press down (see figure 3).

4. Cut the second strip and sew it along the second side of the centre square, overlapping the first strip at one end (see figure 4).

5. Continue working around the square with each successive layer of material, overlapping at the corners to cover the whole foundation square (see figure 5).

This is the basic method for log-cabin piecing. I have used other variations to create more organic shapes in pieced backgrounds including:
• Joining tiny scraps into strips before using these strips to assemble the square.
• Using raw edges and visible thread to create the block.
• Making the strips in irregular shapes, subverting the straight lines.

Opposite: Cotton scraps are tacked to wool gauze using a distorted log-cabin method.

Left: The completed sample is overstitched with dense white, silk running stitches (30 x 20cm / 12 x 8in).

The sample above shows a piece of wool gauze tacked to a foundation fabric and decorated with an interpretation of log-cabin patchwork.

The basics of this method are simple to master. You are then left with a foundation-piecing technique that can be used in different ways.

In stage 1, shown left, naturally dyed wool gauze is topped with scraps of cotton. I have pieced unevenly, using the raw edges rather than stitching on the underside to conceal the join. The scraps are not uniform in size and so subvert the square, leaving it looking more organic. I have simply tacked down the edges.

Stage 2, pictured above, is an extension of the previous work. I have consolidated the pieced background by using dense overstitching in white silk thread and a simple cross shape to cover the pieced fabrics. It has added a stability and solidity to the piece of work, the small scraps of cloth partly concealed beneath the stitching.

Part four:
Contemplative

Reflective and mindful practice

It is so hard to slow down to the pace where it is possible to explore one's mind.

***Writings**, Agnes Martin*

Above and right:

12 Summer Days, 18 Winter Days (2014). Naturally dyed wool gauze. The title refers to the test times used traditionally by dyers to test light fastness (50 x 24cm / 19¾ x 9½in).

Slow making using textiles has a special quality. It is a process that is generative and makes something, useful or maybe not, in a slow process of growth. I see stitching as a common language with the ability to relax, unite and inspire. Stitching and other textile techniques (knitting, weaving) can create something called the 'relaxation response'. This is a measurable state identified by Harvard Medical School Professor Herbert Benson that introduces a feeling of calm and is characterized by lowered blood pressure, heart rate and muscle tension.

Many artists and makers describe the sensation of being 'in the zone' when working – a happy place where the creative process is a smooth and reflexive experience. Mihaly Csikszentmihalyi identifies this as 'flow', a state in which you are fully engaged with a task, challenged by your work, in a manner that is not stressful but satisfying. The process of being in a state of 'flow' can be very sustaining to an artist. The combination of engagement with materials, using one's hands and the level of absorption in an activity can be highly therapeutic. Processes that employ engagement between hands and brain have a way of progressing in a calm way. If I think about the repetitive rhythms of hand stitch, I feel an emphasis on the process, often not the end product – a strong connection to the feel of the fabric, the choice of thread, the way the cloth moves as I work my needle through it. The pace of this can lead to a measured way of thinking and often not only about the work in hand. Meaning can emerge from the making process, the repetition and rhythm forming a restorative activity.

Chase Devil Sutra (2014)

This piece of work was developed using wool gauze, silk fabrics and threads that had been dyed at different times of year using just one plant, *Hypericum perforatum* or St John's Wort. Another common name for the plant is 'Chase Devil', which refers to its use as a medicinal herb to treat depression and low mood. The heavily overstitched surface is a meditation on this, the 'sutra' of the title used in Buddhism to refer to 'a thread that holds things together'.

Above: Wool and silk scraps dyed with *Hypericum perforatum.*

Right: Detail of dense overstitching. The threads were dyed with the fabrics to unify the colours.

Opposite: *Chase Devil Sutra* (2014). Wool and silk on wool blanket (25 x 25cm / 10 x 10in).

Roz Hawker

Roz Hawker is an Australian artist who uses a number of media in her practice including hand stitch. She describes the internal peace she needs to be able to stitch and of needing a quiet place inside herself. She uses naturally dyed cloth, thread and hand stitching to imbue her fabrics with a sense of time, 'the possibility of stillness, and the meditative and restorative quality that time holds. Repetition, building of layers of fragility and openness; all are evident in the cloth, in the landscape and in our lives.' The process of stitching and reconnecting with herself this way is described as being able to breathe more slowly again.

Below: *Quiet Conversation* (2011) by Roz Hawker. Naturally dyed silk cloth and thread.

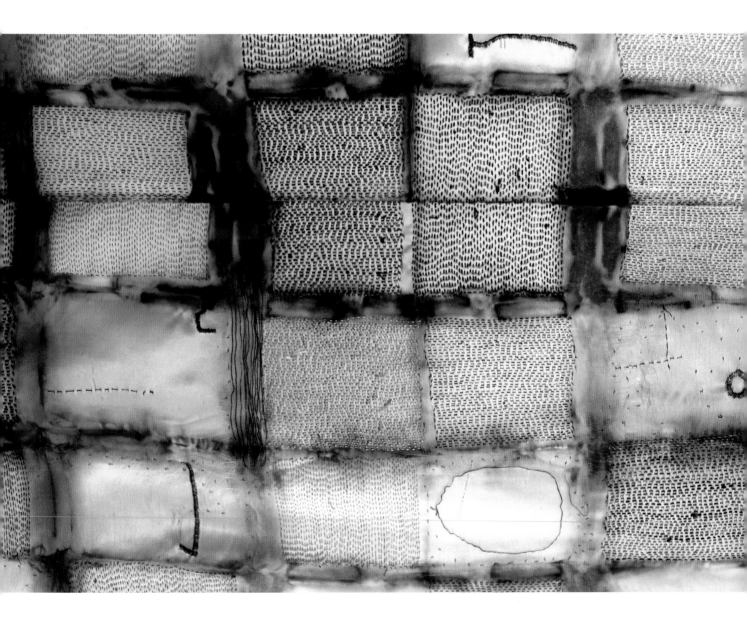

Roanna Wells

Above: Untitled work by Roanna Wells. Herringbone stitch on wool (35 x 25cm / 13¾ x 10in).

Roanna's practice has evolved from a love of collecting and arranging, taking time and precision through repetitive processes of mark-making, to create detailed, often graphic works in drawing and hand embroidery. Using a very minimal colour palette and choosing only one or two techniques at a time, the works have a meditative and absorbing quality, simple and focused.

The time-consuming nature of hand embroidery, along with its permanence and integration with the surface fabric, expresses a commitment and dedication to the production, giving depth and gravitas.

Stitch journals – a regular practice

'I love that time is a material' –
Judy Martin

Above: *Stitch Journal* (2012, ongoing). Recycled linen cloth and hand stitch using hand-dyed threads.

Left: Stitching the journal.

Many artists use a journal or sketchbook as part of their daily art practice. These can be used for recording images, textures or words, or as a tool for developing work.

I find that my most productive thinking time is accompanied by needle, thread and cloth. In a particularly hectic period of my life, I discovered a direct correlation between problem solving and the time I spent stitching. My daily practice – a stitch journal – developed at this time. For me it is a mixture of seasonal observation and thinking space. My stitches are sometimes inspired by a snapshot of the season or some colour found in the view from a window. However, the project is process based and a useful tool to get ideas flowing.

When stitching, I try to clear my head. I use the time to be as present as I can be in that moment. The work grows slowly and fabric is added when it is needed. Stitches are made using a mixture of threads – often hand-dyed, but of different weights. I often layer new stitches over existing ones.

As I continue to use this journal, I recognize less obvious outcomes. It has become a starting point for more resolved pieces of work, as it creates a sense of place – the stitches rooted in the locality where they were made. The repetitious nature of the work has improved my mastery of stitch technique and allows me to pick up the rhythms of my stitches quickly. On the busiest days, I find a window of time, even if it is only a few minutes, to pick up the cloth and continue.

Judy Martin

Above: *Not To Know But To Go On* (2013) by Judy Martin (6899 x 35.5cm / 226 x 1ft).

Canadian textile artist Judy Martin uses the idea of daily practice in her monumental work *Not To Know But To Go On* (the name of the piece taken from the writings of artist Agnes Martin). For three years she used her practice as one might use the daily ritual of writing a diary. The design of the piece refers to her Finnish cultural heritage of rag-rug making (although the piece is stitched, not woven). Every day one complete skein of stranded cotton embroidery thread was couched over strips of found fabric from her own collection on to a cotton canvas backing. She says, 'Stitching gets me up in the morning, I look forward to spending that quiet time with myself ... It's emotional therapy; as I stitch, other things fall into place; the time it takes helps me to be quiet; inner time goes backwards and forwards. Time is recycled.'

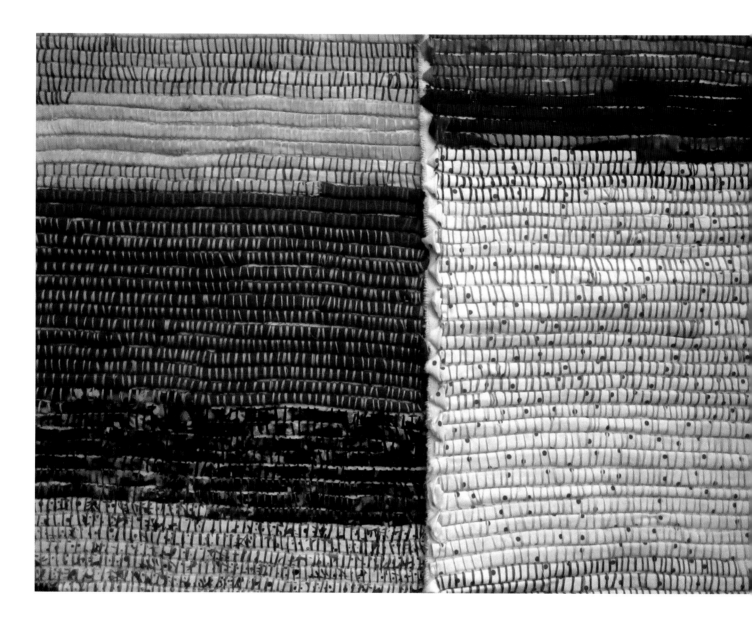

Above: *Not To Know But To Go On* (2013), detail.

This 'private and controlled endeavour', as Judy describes it, speaks to me as a visible record of time, making it tangible. It is a dense, material representation of thought and making. There is great craftsmanship visible in the repetition exhibited in the work. As I look at the densely stitched loops and coils of this work, so great in length after three years of daily stitching, I wish I could touch it and properly engage with the physicality of the object. Judy says, 'I'm interested in producing something very simple and quiet and marked repeatedly with the human hand. Not because it's a metaphor for anything, but just because it's an object that says, unequivocally, I was here; I spent time with this; feel my touch.'

Beginning a stitch journal

Materials:
- Cloth – choose one with a handle that you like. Wool, linen or cotton would work well. The cloth needs to be strong enough to accept different types of thread and dense stitching. See how easy it is to pass your threaded needle through the cloth, and, if it is a struggle, consider using something else. Rhythmic, repetitive stitching is difficult to achieve if the weave is too tight or the fabric stiff.
- Needle and a selection of threads – I like to use different weights and fibres and the threads I hand dye.
- Embroidery hoop, if you use one.
- A marking tool, this could be your needle, a water-soluble pen, or hera marker, although these are not essential.

Things to consider when beginning a stitch journal
- A time frame: Daily, weekly, monthly or as and when the mood takes you.
- A theme, or trigger for your work. A section of my own journal is made up of daily circles, each a colour swatch in stitch of the sky that day, as I observed it in the morning. A wash of pale greys, whites and the occasional blue that records the northern sky where I live.
- A shape to work with, or within. This could be a square or a circle, or something more pictorial. Draw or mark it on to the fabric using your needle, hera marker or water-soluble pen. Alternatively, you could visualise the area you want to stitch and simply begin.
- Stitch choices. Running stitch is a good starting point, but you could choose something from your stitch vocabulary or decide to master something new. Stitches with 'movement' will have a different feel to a stand-alone stitch, such as a French knot. Students attending an evening class that I teach decided that they would use a journal format as a stitch challenge, mastering new stitches and recording the results.
- Reflection. As you work on your journal, reflect on your colour choices, the feel of the materials, the time taken.
- Adaptation. When you next pick up the work, you could decide to start where you left off or begin to stitch a new area of cloth. You may find yourself revisiting areas at a later time, unpicking, reworking, adapting, layering.
- There is no projected outcome for this type of record keeping, but you will have developed a very personal on-going piece of slow stitching to use and return to as you wish, and carved out some time and space in your daily routine.

Left: A section from my *Stitch Journal* – a circle was stitched daily after observing the colour of the sky.

Stitching, walking, mapping

To walk is to journey in the mind, as much as the land: it is deeply meditative.
Being Alive, Tim Ingold

Walking is more often than not the slower option when getting from A to B. It is also a great space for thinking. The pace of your thinking can fall into a pattern with your steps, allowing an opportunity for problem solving and observation. Being outside is also well known for its restorative benefits. Just seeing pictures of green spaces has been shown to speed recovery in hospital patients and a ten-minute local walk per day has been shown to have health benefits. Psychologists Rachel and Stephen Kaplan write of the effect of 'soft fascinations', for example observing cloud formations or leaves falling from the trees, as a useful tool for stress reduction. Fully engaging with a place is a slow process and it demands your attention.

Above and right: Pieced and stitched evocations of place. The fabrics are often dyed with plants from those locations.

Walking as a practice

In my practice, I have recently spent two years exploring the area around a now-demolished dye-works (once the largest in the world) in the city where I live. The work is inspired by investigations, archive research and community-based projects. I have begun a regular walking practice around the perimeter of the site, now a post-industrial wasteland, overgrown with weeds, or rather plants out of place. Rosebay willowherb, hawthorn, wild currant, buddleia and yarrow all flourish unchecked and these plants have become my palette of dyes for both wool and thread. Regional variations in this type of liminal plant life, local soil and historical human activity all impact on the colour produced.

Above and below: The walking route along the dye-works path reveals many plants to be used as dyes from this location.

Above: Stitch sketches
in my sketchbook.

Below: Samples,
photographs and plant
material from my
sketchbook.

I collect these plant materials on my walks and the dyes are worked and absorbed gradually
into locally produced cloth. Embedded stitches echo my walking patterns around the site,
stitching themselves into the landscape. I have observed changes to the place month by month,
slowly becoming more acquainted with the area.

When working in this way, I think of 'mapping' as creating a personal impression of a place –
built up slowly over time and during repeated visits. This contrasts with a pictorial or illustrative
version of the place as it actually appears. I have used the following methods when working in
this way: stitch sketches, colour mapping, using maps, written thoughts.

Stitch sketches

Made on location with a needle and thread, stitch sketches are an addition to the photographic records I make alongside. Using small woollen base squares and a needle and thread, this is quick reflexive way of recording. I can then develop these small pieces at home, considering the thread and fabric choices that might be most significant. I collage these fabrics, often hand-dyed, found, or significant to the area I am exploring, into small-scale 'maps' that for me create a representation of that place.

Above and below: Stitch sketches made on location. Closer examination reveals the tiny stitches in the thread sketch.

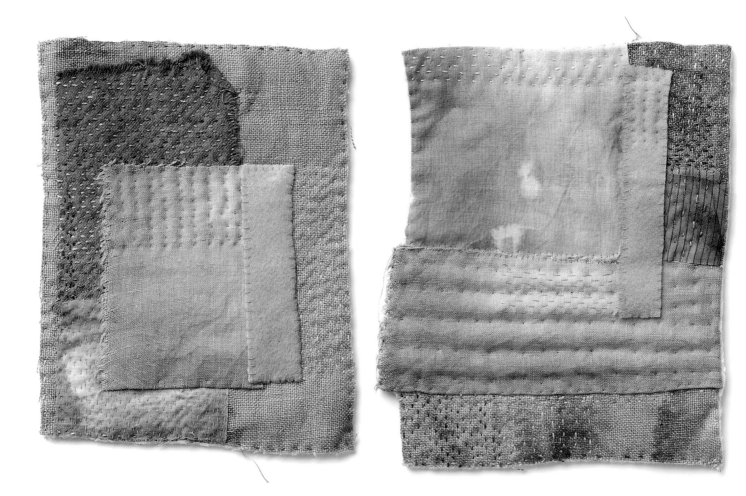

Colour mapping

Above and right:
Plant-dyed wool and linen
found fabrics and hand
stitch. The purple colour
is created using logwood
– a dye much used in the
area during the nineteenth
century (13 x 16cm /
5 x 6¼in).

I look for found colour on my walks. This is sometimes, literally, collected from the ground – paint
chips, interesting leaves, tickets, wood and metal scrap, and other ephemera, even discarded
cloth. Or it can be colour discovered by observation: contrasts in foliage, the brightness of the
sky on that day, changes in local graffiti altering a familiar view, the green biofilms that grow on
buildings and stone walls. I also collect colour as plant material to use for dyes. Colours from
nature can work together in surprising ways. I'm thinking of the acid bright of mosses on the
moors near where I live, and how they contrast sharply with the greys of the sky and the dark
heather and tussock grass in the winter months. This palette is echoed in the colours and tones
that can be created in a dye pot. Thinking about and recording the qualities of the natural colours
around you can be a good precursor to starting a slow project inspired by a place.

Using maps, examining pathways and walking routes

I particularly like the idea of desire paths or lines, pathways that develop over time when people
adopt them as shortcuts by foot. They could cut across or around your work as stitches – the
rhythms and regularity of your movements, and directional nature of stitch whilst making them,
like slow steps as you walk.

Written reflection

I find this is a useful way of recording changes to a place and examining a site. An example from my sketchbook: 'Dyeworks path walk, through viaduct arch. Filthy day, pouring rain, deserted. That strange stillness of the New Year. New rubbish fly-tipped this time. Looking closely at vegetation – what grows where, taking back the landscape. Collected weeds – ragwort, cleavers, club moss that were all extended over tarmac repairs like a green carpet. Found fabric scraps submerged in mud. Added to my collection, heavy with Yorkshire sandstone, rinse and repeat, rinse and repeat.' Looking back at my description, I am taken back to that day in a way that simply using a photograph as a trigger would not have achieved.

Below: Found fabrics and reflective writing in my sketchbook.

Christine Mauersberger

Christine Mauersberger is an artist based in Cleveland, Ohio, USA. She describes her densely stitched works as maps. 'They are not maps that you would recognize, and most people wouldn't. The map for me is where every map is a walk through my thought. I try to use natural materials and also use recycled materials – old blanket that feels good – but I also like that the cloth has a previous life and I'm giving it another life. I'm trying to take the humble, ubiquitous stitch and create a three-dimensional space where you could walk through it and explore, so that the beauty of the stitch comes out.' Her work, like the pieces by Judy Martin, is concerned with the marking of time. 'Time is both a real and abstract concept. My challenge is to make artwork that expresses a passing of moments by using sewing as the medium. Each single line of thread ... in the work serves as an artifact and a record of the passing of time.'

Above: *Mind Map* (2011) by
Christine Mauersberger.
Hand-stitched silk/cotton on
linen (104 x 101cm / 41 x 39¾in).

Hannah Lamb

Below and right:
Linear Mapping (2014)
by Hannah Lamb.

Hannah Lamb is an artist and academic based in the UK whose practice uses textiles, photography and installation. She observes the landscape through a variety of methods, including regular walks along a stretch of the River Aire in West Yorkshire. Found objects from her walks are incorporated in pieces that ask questions about our connection to local landscapes.

'Walking is a key element of my practice. It forms part of my research process, enabling me to observe and experience my environment. Making similar walks at different times and seasons I observe subtle changes in myself and the landscape. The speed of my walking might be influenced by weather conditions and the observed flora and fauna may vary from day to day.

The installation called *Linear Mapping* (2014) represents a series of walks taking place over a period of several months and in two different areas: the Aire Valley, near my home in Cottingley, West Yorkshire, and Great Missenden, Bucks. Both are areas I know well and share similar beech woodlands. They also have significant differences and are loaded with personal and emotional resonances for me.

Linear Mapping aims to capture and record a number of purposeful walks in the form of a collection of threads or strands, each one representing a walk. The threads are made in different ways, twisting, knitting, stitching, and use stitch and plant stains to introduce mark and colour. I stitch in an intuitive manner, making an abstract mark that suggests a sense of time and place. I use a kind of visual shorthand that is personal to me and represents my being a part of the landscape.

Walking has the power to transform our daily lives through slowing down and appreciating our world. My practice aims to develop a greater awareness of our relationship with the environment, understanding our place in the world through walking and making.'

Stitching community: communal projects, wellbeing and health

'Alone we can do so little, together we can do so much.'
Helen Keller

Above: Hand stitching for reflection at a mindful making workshop.

Right and above right: Naye Subah quilt (2011). A Hive/Naye Subah project.

Projects concerned with the wellbeing and mental health of participants have been a big part of my work over the last ten years. My personal understanding of the restorative aspects of slow textile work have developed over this time, as I have had the opportunity to share different techniques and observe the different responses that individuals and groups have to them. I have also observed, in most environments, that when people are engaged in a making activity, they are far more likely to relax and have meaningful conversations with their peers. Textile activities address commonality – themes, stories, symbols – that work across cultures and for all people. Slow methodologies can be even more powerful, as they can look at seasonality, place and time as triggers for communal work.

Mindfulness and making

In wellbeing and mental-health settings in recent years, a popular therapeutic technique has been that of mindfulness training. This uses aspects of meditation, breathing exercises and yoga, emphasizing a state of being 'in the moment' or looking at one's present experience with complete attention to it. Being in this state helps with observation skills and in noticing details of the things around us at that time. Bringing our focus into the now means it is difficult to worry about what is coming in the future or what has been in the past. The benefits can include helping with relaxation, concentration and physical ill-health conditions, and a reduction in anxiety, stress and depression.

As a textile-based practitioner, I was particularly interested in how making techniques, particularly stitch-based, would fit with the processes of mindfulness training. I have explored 'mindful making' in group sessions, based on the idea that individual stitches could be seen as an in-breath and an out-breath. At a monthly slow stitching group I facilitate, we combine textile-mending techniques with conversations about mindfulness and enjoyment of the process.

Above: Making patchwork using English paper-piecing techniques.

The combination of repairing items with emotional significance and a focus on the present is very powerful. Mindful stitching offers an opportunity to exercise quiet making in a supportive environment. Conversations flowed between participants but also felt like conversations with the materials used too. The repetitive aspects of hand stitching offered a calming and thoughtful head space, and yet gave those participants an opportunity to engage in a generative, productive making activity.

At a mental health project, traditional patchwork techniques using the English paper-piecing method stimulated some interesting discussions in a group. Connections were made between the mindfulness training that participants engaged with as part of their therapeutic regimen and the slow craft of patchwork. It was agreed in the group that the repetitive aspect of paper-piecing, the pleasure found in handling and choosing fabrics, and the concentration required proved to be an excellent distraction from debilitating, anxious thoughts. The group, none of whom had tried patchwork before, also enjoyed the zero-waste aspect of patchwork, and began to swap fabric scraps and old clothes to increase their collections of materials. The group was in agreement that it was initially hard to adjust to a slow pace of working, but that it felt very rewarding to our mental health and wellbeing when we did.

Seed to fabric projects

Above: Dye-plant harvest at Hive.

I have managed several community-based projects that have developed the idea of whole-process working. These initially began as a project called 'Out There' for community arts charity Hive as part of a funding programme called 'Ecominds' developed by the mental-health charity Mind, as an award partner of the Big Lottery Fund. The project focused on research that showed the benefits to wellbeing that regular contact with green spaces gave, particularly for people experiencing mental-health distress. I devised a programme of activities around the creation of a dye-plant and fibre garden at a local allotment site, with the idea of growing plants from seed, processing them and using the dyed fibres and fabrics in collaborative group textile sessions. A weekly walk to the plot, some light horticultural activity, and a chat in the open air proved to be a simple but effective format through all but the worst winter weather. The project developed as a firmly seasonal activity, something that in an urban environment can be difficult to achieve. A gentle reminder of the seasons and natural processes can really enhance wellbeing. Feedback from participants echoes this view; as one of them put it 'It was great to find local walks I didn't know about and a chance to work on an allotment, seeing changes through the seasons. This project gave me the chance to experiment and play with materials, colours and techniques, while working in a helpful and easy atmosphere.'

Sow: Sew

Sow: Sew, a community-made work, was assembled by many hands using fabrics dyed at community dye-garden projects. The gardens were made as part of a project called 'The Fabric of Bradford', funded by the Heritage Lottery Fund (2012–2014). Participants explored the textile dyeing heritage of their city through reminiscing, hands-on activities and research. Towards the end of the project participants were given a pack of materials, all dyed using plants grown during the project, or harvested locally. They were given the challenge of assembling them on

Below: *Sow: Sew* (2014) on display at a community dye garden.

to a background square using any method they chose. Some chose log-cabin-style designs and pieced their work on to the background cloth, but many other methods were also used by the sixty people who took part. There were initial comments about the lack of choice (you could only use the fabric that had been supplied) which at first was seen as limiting, but later many saw this as a liberating experience.

Below: Detail from *Sow: Sew* (2014).

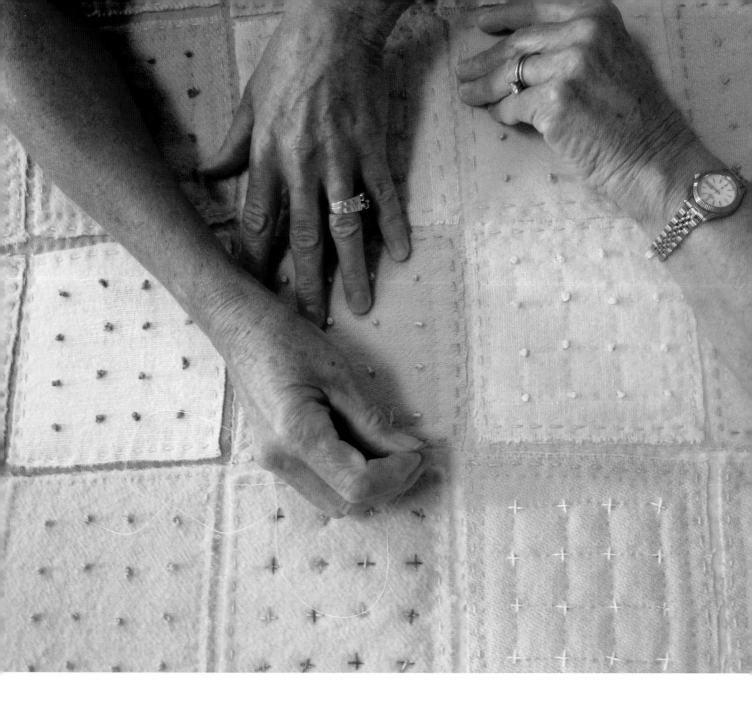

The Manitoulin Circle Project

Above: Working on *Layers of Time* (2009–2013), Manitoulin Circle Project.

Canadian artist Judy Martin (see page 96) worked with over 140 people during the four-year Manitoulin Circle Project. Four large 'meditation panels' were created during the project: *Earth Ark*, *Precious Water*, *Layers of Time* and *Mended World*. Each panel carries the message of environmental appreciation and reparation. The work was largely made from donated and charity-shop materials: damask tablecloths and other domestic textiles, including crocheted doilies, women's handkerchiefs and wool blankets. A theme of re-creation and also of reparation through the remaking of these materials ran through the project. Every week during the four years of the project participants gathered in a church hall to work on the pieces, building community and personal friendships, as they slowly created their pieces of work.

The *Mended World* panel is constructed using a string-piecing technique. Using a sewing machine, four or five long narrow strips of a variety of textured damasks (from recycled tablecloths) were sewn together along their long edges to create a new striped fabric. This fabric is then re-cut several times and sewn back together to make a wide piece of new fabric.

The project speaks of time and has produced beautiful, meaningful work. As an artist who works with communities, I am always deeply moved when I think about the 'other' work that goes into producing pieces like this. The other work is the conversation, the communication, the slowly getting to know one's stitching neighbour, the memories and skills shared, and the hours of committed thought and organization of the facilitator/artist. Somehow the tactile cloth holds all of this within its folds, layers and stitches. This work is a reminder that people and places mixed together, and the exchanges they have, can produce satisfying results.

Below: *Mended World* (2012) (244 x 244cm / 96 x 96in) a panel from the Manitoulin Circle Project.

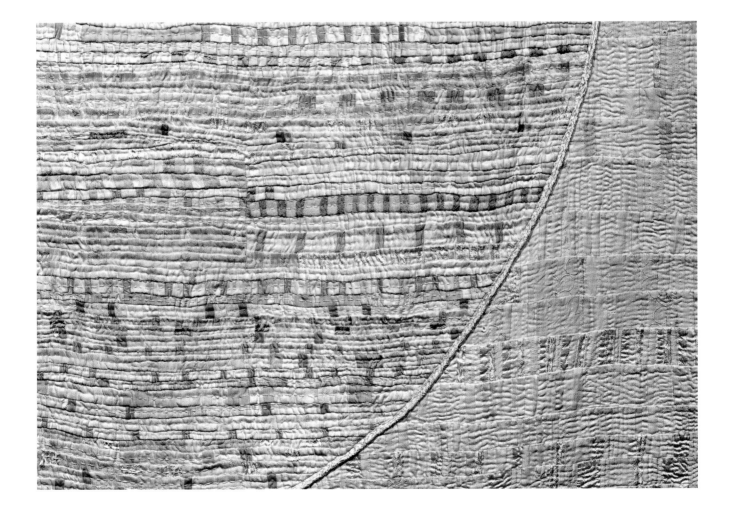

Narratives through cloth

Below: *Community Cloth*
(2012–2014), designed
and stitched by Creative
Threads group. A map of
the group meeting place
and words picked by the
participants are included
(200 x 70cm / 79 x 27½in).

Textiles are evocative objects. However ordinary or mundane, they have a power to remind us of times of significance in our lives. Tablecloths, family heirlooms, tea towels, things collected on our holidays all carry stories and memories. I work frequently with groups of women who are originally from the South Asian diaspora. In our sessions, I encourage the participants to bring in their own favourite textile pieces to use and to discuss the stories and memories associated with them. I learned shisha mirror work as part of a materials and techniques exchange with one participant, and once received the gift of a Nepalese spinning wheel, handmade from skip timber, from a participant in a heritage project. 'Talking textiles' is a great way to explore cultural similarities and differences, but even more so when groups are engaging in textile projects alongside story telling and listening. Working with textiles can provide security in a group environment, a place that is pleasurable to be in and can provide comfort too.

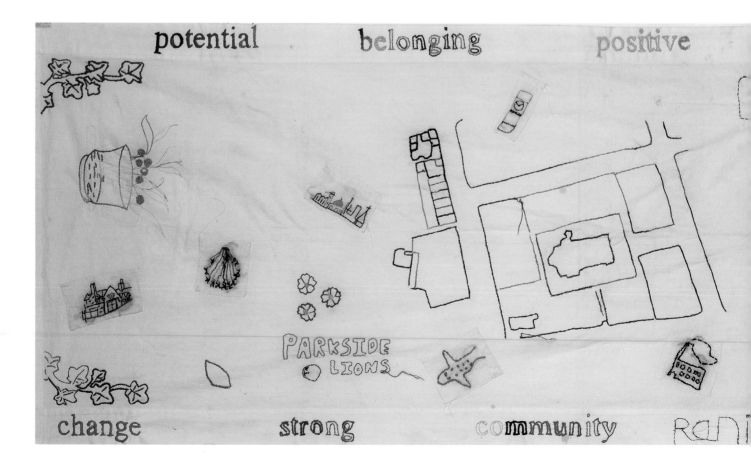

Above: *Community Cloth*, detail. 'There's a story in every pocket in this community' commented one stitcher.

Conclusion

'Slow stitching: absorbing, soothing, satisfying, intriguing.'

Project participant

This book is not designed to provide a blueprint for projects, but to act as an overview of some of the ideas that I see as central to slow, creative textile methodologies. I want to encourage a perspective that sees us make small shifts in our perspective of 'whole process' working. This can include a broad spectrum of making, including consideration of our materials and their provenance, thinking about traditional and cultural attributes of textiles and their meaning to us, and reflecting on the textile projects we are involved in, whether individual or communal. I see the themes of Slow Movements around the world as optimistic. For textiles, this can change the way we look at and appreciate textiles around us, how we work with them, and understand the connections and stories we have in common.

Above and left: Work in progress – a log-cabin inspired sample on white handkerchief.

Useful suppliers

Fabrics

Organic Cotton Fabrics Ltd.
www.organiccotton.biz
Fairtrade and organic fabrics.

Greenfibres
www.greenfibres.com
Organic and sustainable fabric, wadding and sewing threads.

Fair Trade Fabric
www.fairtradefabric.co.uk
Organic, fairtrade cotton by the metre.

Threads

Texere Yarns
www.texere-yarns.co.uk
Large selection of yarns and threads for dyeing.

Wild Colours
www.wildcolours.co.uk
Natural dyestuffs and mordants.

The Textile Society

The society holds two antique textiles fairs every year in the UK – a great source of inspiration and somewhere to purchase unusual secondhand materials from all over the world.
www.textilesociety.org.uk

Right: An ongoing recording of weathered fabric samples (60 x 30cm / 23½ x 11¾in)

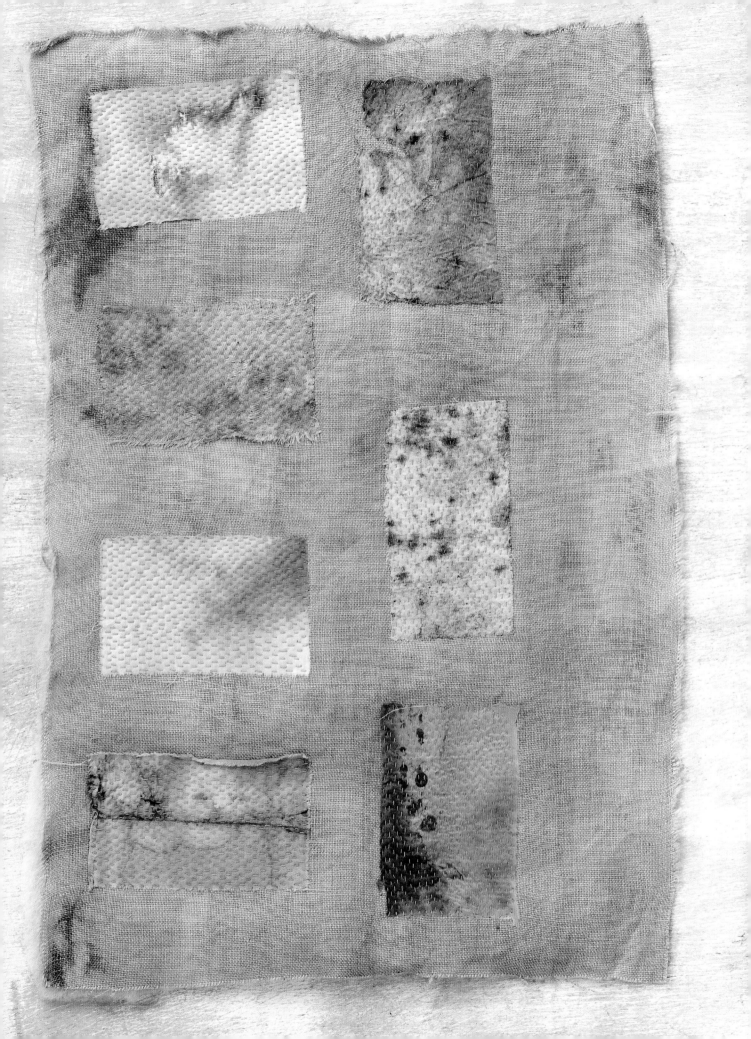

Further Reading

Albers, Anni, *On Designing* (Wesleyan University Press, 1962)

Arnett, William et al, *The Quilts of Gees Bend* (Tinwood, 2002)

Celant, Germano, *Louise Bourgeois: The Fabric Works* (Skira, 2010)

Dean, Jenny, *Wild Colour* (Mitchell Beazley, 1999)

Felcey, Helen (editor), Ravetz, Amanda (editor) and Kettle, Alice (editor), 2013 *Collaboration Through Craft* (Berg, 2013)

Gale, Colin, and Jasbir Kaur, *The Textile Book* (Bloomsbury Academic, 2002)

Gauntlett, David, *Making is Connecting: The Social Meaning of Creativity, from DIY and Knitting to YouTube and Web 2.0.* (Polity, 2011)

Gillow, John, and Sentance, Colin, *World Textiles: A Visual Guide to Traditional Techniques* (Thames & Hudson, 2004)

Gordon, Beverly, *Textiles: The Whole Story: Uses, Meanings, Significance* (Thames & Hudson, 2011)

Holmes, Cas, *The Found Object in Textile Art* (Batsford, 2010)

Honoré, Carl, *In Praise of Slow: How a Worldwide Movement is Challenging the Cult of Speed* (Orion, 2004)

Ingold, Tim, *Being Alive: Essays on Movement, Knowledge and Description* (Routledge, 2011)

Kettle, Alice, and McKeating, Jane, *Hand Stitch, Perspectives* (Bloomsbury, 2012)

Koren, Leonard, *Wabi-sabi: For Artists, Designers, Poets & Philosophers* (Imperfect Publishing, 2008)

Koide, Yukiko and Tsuzuki, Kyoichi, *Boro: Rags and Tatters from the Far North of Japan* (Aspect Corp, 2009)

Lippard, Lucy R., The Lure of the Local: Senses of Place in a Multicentered Society (New Press, 1997)

Millar, Leslie et.al., *Cloth and Memory Vol 2.* (Salts Estates Ltd, 2013)

Payne, Sheila, *Embroidered Textiles: A World Guide to Traditional Patterns* (Thames and Hudson, 1990)

Snook, Barbara Lilian, *Embroidery Stitches* (Batsford, 1963)

Solnit, Rebecca, *Wanderlust: A History of Walking* (Verso, 2006)

Turkle, Sherry, *Evocative Objects: Things We Think With* (MIT Press, 2007)

Zaman, Niaz, *The Art of Kantha Embroidery* (Bangladesh Shilpnkala Academy, 1981)

Left: Old scraps, overdyed with walnut dye and embedded with stitches to create a new surface.

Index

Acknowlegements

I would like to thank the following:

Joy Hart and all at Hive.

WEA Yorkshire and Humberside, Naye Subah Project, West Bowling Creative Threads.

National Lottery for supporting community projects mentioned in the text.

Sue, Mary, Cath, Vikki and Pat for stitching squares.

Hannah, most excellent critical friend.

Blog readers and workshop attenders for all your insight and helpful feedback.

Kristy Richardson and Batsford for supporting this book.

Michael Wicks for the wonderful photography.

David, Alice, Eleanor, Martha, Frieda and Scout without whom ...

This book is for Mum and Dad; thank you for everything.

Picture Credits